The Life and Times of Sam Mihara

As told to Alexandra Villarreal

The Life and Times of Sam Mihara

as told to Alexandra Villarreal

Second Edition 2022, Second Printing, Published in the United States in 2022 by

Mihara Associates, www.sammihara.com

Story inspired by the experiences of Sam Mihara. Written by Alexandra Villarreal

Printed and bound in Santa Ana, California, USA

Table of Contents

To the ancestors who suffer to give their survivors a better life, and to the kids who know what it means to be jailed for a life you never chose.

Foreword

After a bitter three-year experience at a desolate prison camp in Northern Wyoming, I wanted nothing to do with the injustice and pain caused by my government and its supporters. So, following guidance from my parents, I focused on getting a good education and succeeded in a very satisfying 42-year career with the Boeing Company.

But following retirement in 1997, I was casting about for a new endeavor. I was traveling and fly fishing around the world when I received a call that changed my entire outlook on life. The call was in 2011 from a group at the former prison site in Wyoming, called Heart Mountain Wyoming Foundation (HMWF).

The person on the other line said they received a request from the Department of Justice of the U.S. government. The DOJ attorneys were holding a lawyers' conference and wanted to have someone with experience in the camp give a talk. That was my first attempt to recall the events that my family and I lived through long ago.

The results were very positive — the lead attorney at the conference immediately sent a message to all U.S. Attorney offices to invite me to speak.

After that, I continued developing my story and gave more talks. I added historical context, and focused on the bottom line — can it happen again to others?

The speaking engagements grew to reach more than 50,000 students, teachers, lawyers and parents – people who knew very little about the history of a massive injustice against a single race, but who were willing to learn.

When I toured, I asked my audiences what improvements I could make to my storytelling. The most frequent response was that I should prepare a book that summarized highlights of my experience. Most books on this topic are limited to either fiction or non-fiction events involving a personal experience at the camp. Other books are limited to the major legal and historical events, such as unconstitutional laws, executive orders, and congressional actions. I wanted to offer something different.

I wanted a book that could help everyone understand the major events that took place in my life, along with a summary of the government's decisions along the way – both the bad and the good.

I hope you enjoy reading about what I remember and wish only that you pass on this story to others. Then, they can, in turn, pass it on, so eventually everyone will understand why I feel so strongly that mass imprisonment should never happen again – to anyone.

Best wishes, Sam Mihara

The Life and Times of Sam Mihara

A great nation does not hide history.

— President George W. Bush

Danger!

Its body was about a quarter inch wide and long, bloated with blood and cloaked in brown.

At first, I thought it was a spider. We had spiders back in San Francisco, and I knew what they were about — frightening, but at least familiar.

Then, I remembered the warning signs. A few weeks before, one of the departments had come up with posters to display around camp, in both English and Japanese. There had been a lot of fine print — too much to read, much less remember. But a few words flashed back in my mind: "Danger," and "Rocky Mountain Spotted Fever."

I didn't know anything about "Rocky Mountain Spotted Fever," except that it was somehow connected to "danger." And so I sat there in shock, having a staring contest with the tick embedded in my inner thigh, though I didn't even know what a tick was at the time.

It all happened around 8 p.m., in the first six months after arriving at Heart Mountain. It was time for bed, again, and as I removed my underwear, I didn't feel a thing. But I saw it. And I tugged on it. And part of its body came out, but the rest stayed.

So I called my mom. And she called an ambulance. When I got to the makeshift hospital, the doctor told me I had acted all wrong.

"You should never remove a tick manually," he said. "It was in the posters. You should have known."

The doctor didn't waste time on anesthesia. Instead, he took his scalpel and started digging, rounding up the pieces and parts my own surgery had missed. I don't remember how long it took—probably 20 or 30 minutes—but I do remember exactly how it felt. Like when you get cut by a knife, but again and again, over and over.

I was just a kid. Seven decades later, I can still feel the scalpel — how it burned.

My mom was there, supervising, concerned but never nervous or excited. Somehow, regardless of the hardships we went through, she always held herself together.

Whether my father came, I couldn't tell you. I wouldn't be surprised if Mom chose not to bother him. By then, he was already going blind, and an emergency trip to the hospital was not in the cards.

Anyways, the doctor removed what was left of the tick. I didn't get Rocky Mountain Spotted Fever, so I went back to my normal life.

If you could call it that. For me, "life as normal" for three years of my childhood meant unknown diseases and dangerous flora and fauna. It meant being caged in by a fence, with guards in their towers pointing rifles at targets like me. It meant freezing cold cells that were 20x20 feet, so the whole family was crammed into a space with no room to breathe.

And it meant leaving home in San Francisco for a more bitter piece of the West, where I wasn't wanted — and where I didn't want to be.

To this day, the worst part of it all is that I hadn't done anything to deserve Heart Mountain. I was an innocent Japanese-American citizen, a child. My singular crime was an ancestral culture.

But in 1942, that was enough for the federal government.

Part 1: Getting There

Blind

The guards told us to close our blinds. We were on a trip to nowhere, and we couldn't even look out the window.

Sequestered and supervised on a moving train, for us, a view of the outside never would have meant an escape plan. But as we traveled along unfamiliar railway to an unknown destination, it could have given the stability of foreshadowing as the terrain turned darker and colder and California faded into the distance.

At least, we could have been slightly more prepared for what was to come.

The reason why open blinds were barred had nothing to do with us, and everything to do with them — the real Americans still living in the real world, going along with their daily lives. For them, a train filled with only Japanese Americans traveling cross-country might have been alarming, even before reports of Holocaust labor and death camps hit newsstands. And so with our blinds, we shielded them from the nasty reality we were living. They would never have to know. As our train chugged along, they didn't even have to think twice.

But I'm getting ahead of myself. Let me rewind.

Sam Mihara in 1939, Courtesy of the Mihara Family Collection

I was born in San Francisco a Nisei: A second generation Japanese American who was provided a comfortable life by the first. But really, our pathway to the United States tracks back to a generation before, when my grandparents decided to break out of the same social strata where our family had lingered for decades. To do that, they knew my father was the answer — him, and his education. My grandparents worked hard so that eventually he could go to Waseda University, the equivalent of an Ivy League school in Japan.

There, my father chose to study English out of all things, and when he graduated, he spoke the language better than I did after my own college graduation in the United States. When it came time for him to find a job, he had no trouble getting hired as a writer for a bilingual newspaper, *The New World Sun*.

The publication just so happened to be headquartered in San Francisco, and so the Mihara family moved. My grandfather had already come years before, but my dad brought over my grandmother and the rest. Here in the United States, Dad met and married my mom, and together they had me and my brother — two kids who would always exist on a plane that was both foreign and domestic. Eventually, our dual identities as American and Japanese would force us to the world's edge, incarcerated non-criminals in a country where we were citizens. But at first, the duality made little difference. We lived well.

That's not to say we didn't assimilate a bit. At Waseda, my father — my Otoosan, as we called him — minored in religion, and from his love of Judaism he pulled Abrahamic names. My mother became Esther in public, though we still called her our Okaasan at home. My older brother Nobuo, or Nob, got "Joshua" as a middle name — one he learned to despise and reject. But unlike Nob, I liked my biblical reference, Samuel, as an addendum to my given and family names. When I was a child, everyone called me Kiyoshi, but years later, I chose to be Sam.

By the time I was 9 years old, we had eased into life in the United States and lived in a beautiful Victorian house in San Francisco's Japantown — the kind of home you see in old photos of what San Francisco once was. When I was born, my father had already been at the New World Sun for 13 years; as I grew older, he rose through the ranks and always seemed to be busy. My mother was the one who took care of our home; she ran the household and was always around to punish me when I misbehaved, a frequent occurrence.

When May 5th rolled around, my parents would display our family collection of male dolls and samurai statues and fly a carp fish kite outside our house for Boy's Day, a Japanese holiday that celebrates all the boys just for existing. My Okaasan would make us a special dinner, just like any other holiday.

Mihara family, c. 1937, Courtesy of the Mihara Family Collection

Sam and Nob on Boy's Day, Courtesy of the Mihara Family Collection

And we celebrated the other holidays, too: Christmas, Easter. We inherited the best of both our cultures; we were still Japanese, but our parents taught us to be Americans as well. We embraced what it meant to be Japanese Americans, and unlike some of the other immigrant communities who came to the New World, we never boxed ourselves into a corner or chose to resist change. Our father made sure of that — he wanted us to understand a little bit about everywhere we came from, without ever letting go of who we were.

Growing up, our food also straddled the line between the United States and Japan. Dinner usually meant fresh everything — vegetables, fish, rice. There were Japanese poultry farmers just north of San Francisco, so sometimes we got chicken, eggs, or whole milk. But we still sprinkled in the occasional hamburger for good measure; we were American boys, after all.

On Sundays, we went to church. Most other Japanese families were still Buddhist before the war. But my father knew religion, and he chose the Christian faith for himself in college, and then for us years later. We followed Christian doctrine with devotion, and our weekends teetered between our ethnic community and a new, spiritual one.

Christmas celebration, Courtesy of the Mihara Family Collection

Like with our religion, my father always had a way of breaking through the confines of a single social strata. Yes, some of his friends were Japanese, but others were white and in high places. I remember visiting the laps of luxury where his Anglo lawyer friends lived and ogling at the view. We were welcome there, even though we looked different. We were wanted at some of the highest echelons of American society, alongside prominent attorneys who headed up entire law schools in the area.

In the classroom, I spoke English, but at home we carried on in Japanese much of the time. I attended grammar school at the same institution where the U.S. government tasked photographer Dorothea Lange with taking pictures of Japanese-American tots just before their imprisonment. I don't recall her camera outside my classrooms or on the playground, but a lot of my friends appear in her photographs as they recite the pledge of allegiance — the pledge that told us we belonged.

Dorothea's photos would later represent a time when we did not, in fact, belong in the country where we were born. Today, they show us what children look like just before they become victims. The answer is simple: They look like children.

Young boys at Raphael Weill Grammar School, San Francisco, 1942, Courtesy of National Archives / Dorothea Lange

And back then, I was like any other child. I played pranks. I got middling grades. I liked to make teachers bark from frustration, and I threw away opportunities to prove myself just to inspire a laugh.

When I was around eight years old, each of my classmates was endowed with the tremendous responsibility of ringing the start-of-school bell in the morning. We were older, the school's leadership thought, more mature. We were ready to show the younger kids how to behave.

When it was my turn, I purposefully rang the bell early so I could watch all the teachers scurry and squawk like disheveled geese frightened by a hunter's unexpected shot.

Unsurprisingly, I was in and out of trouble constantly, and none of it seemed to matter. My parents still loved me, there was still good food on the table, and my world was still full and happy. So normal and boring, in fact, that I had to shake things up with mischief and bad behavior just to feel imperfection for a while.

Then, on one winter day in December, everything changed.

I was at the movies when it happened. I can't remember which film, but probably a Western with Gene Autry. As a kid, I was always fond of your classic American hero out West, making order in a land of lawlessness.

Or I guess it could have been an animated feature. Back then, Walt Disney was just getting off the ground. Snow White was still all the rage, and I knew all about it because one of my best friends Willie Ito had loved the movie so much he swore he'd become an animator and work for Walt one day. Pinocchio had just come out as well, and the films swirling from Disney's imagination had captivated my entire generation. They were so quintessentially American — so fresh, and new, and shiny.

Honestly, I can't recall which film I watched on December 7, 1941. Just the headline that followed.

As I came out of the theater, I saw newspapers branded with four big, black words: "Japs Bomb Pearl Harbor." I didn't really know what that meant, or why it would be true. So I ran home to my parents and asked them to explain. They were no help. Even though my Otoosan — my father — was a newsman, he was just as befuddled by the attack as I was.

All we knew was that something that had happened 3,600 miles away might change our lives forever.

See, my parents were documented immigrants, but they weren't American citizens. Their work permits depended not only on job sponsorship, but also on the whims of the U.S. government — which nationalities it decided should qualify for employment-based visas. If a country was a foreign foe, there was always the possibility that its people might be sent back to where they came from. And now that the United States and Japan seemed on the brink of war, our family's future in America looked less bright than just hours before.

Nob and I belonged to this country. We had been born here, and we had never known another home. We understood that our parents could be forced back to Japan, a whole ocean away, as we waited for them here. Dangling above our heads was an axe suspended by the government that could fall at any moment, slicing our family in half. In the shadow of Pearl Harbor, we knew that, and we were afraid.

The next day, on December 8, President Franklin D. Roosevelt came over the airwaves to declare that while I had been watching a movie, "a date which will live in infamy" unfolded on an island I knew almost nothing about. At the time, I was shocked by the body count at Pearl Harbor, how many American GIs had suddenly become casualties in the morning's early hours. As a 9-year-old boy, it was nearly impossible for me to fathom more than 2,000 people dead in an instant when already I could barely wrap my head around what would cause an attack of that magnitude in the first place.

As President Roosevelt gave his famous speech, the question churned around the corners of my mind: What is war, actually?

Soon, I would find out firsthand. War is a force that can make terrible things happen, things that would never be allowed in times of peace.

Things like Executive Order 9066. In theory, FDR's policy didn't target Japanese Americans, or any other race. It was meant to keep anyone from spying for enemy forces in Germany, Italy, and Japan during World War II, or to stop any efforts to sabotage American troops. So technically, it was just as probable that officials would detain huge swathes of German and Italian immigrants on the east coast as the entire Japanese population in the West.

But the east coasters had something on their side that we didn't: They could pass. Europeans had been the original colonists, and Germans and Italians blended better with their puritan neighbors. Meanwhile, our darker skin and Asian visages signaled foreignness to onlookers. We had been the "other" since we arrived in the United States in the late-1860s, and racism had haunted us for decades. Now, that racism finally had a vehicle for realization, and Lieutenant General John DeWitt, who headed up the Western military district in the United States, didn't hesitate. With wartime patriotism on his side, he would make us pay for being different. He targeted anyone with a drop of Japanese blood — even babies and orphans. And no one stopped him.

Soon after December 7, my father began to panic. He knew what was to come — government agents storming in with their long coats and fedoras, looking for evidence of collusion. Paranoid and scared to lose his family, my father began burning papers day and night: Anything that could connect him to his heritage, to the country he had left decades ago. The papers were swallowed by constant fires that were supposed to keep us okay, safe from another kind of flame burning inside the hearts of the white people who lived around us. They had relearned how to hate us; my friends remember our teachers saying that we were responsible for Pearl Harbor, that we were the reason so many Americans had died. But I had been so devastated when FDR had told us about the attack, and I didn't believe that I should feel guilty for something I had mourned myself. I had never stepped foot in Japan, never met a single one of the aggressors. The people who died were my people, not the people who killed them.

I was at school when my father marched to a makeshift office and put our names on a list a few days after FDR backed Executive Order 9066. Despite all his paranoia, he didn't really know what he was doing, but the government did. It needed a head count so when it built our prisons, we would all fit. The U.S. census from two years before was outdated, and officials demanded that representatives of every nearby Japanese-American family visit what used to be a Japanese language school but was now a station devoted to the new policy. My father lined up with the rest of the men and women who never thought to question whether what the government was doing deserved their cooperation. Together, they registered themselves and their loved ones, signing their own fate. Because once they were registered, it was too late. There was no escape.

In Japan, the mentality had always been "don't question, obey." Children are taught that their public officials will behave in a way that reflects their best interest — and that the government always knows best. So when hundreds of thousands of Japanese Americans were asked to identify themselves for a racially-based list mere months after Pearl Harbor, most of them didn't bat an eyelash.

Their government had told them to do it. And their government was always right.

I, for one, knew better. A lot of the young people did. We were American citizens, born and raised, and we understood that we had rights, even if we didn't know the technicalities of what those rights were. Every morning, we stood up in class to recite the words that supposedly defined our Union: "With liberty and justice for all." And in the backs of our minds, we knew this didn't feel like that. Mass registration did not seem like liberty, and paying for the crimes of our race in a home we never knew felt nothing like justice.

There were people who fought back. Fred Korematsu, Gordon Hirabayashi, and Minoru Yasui all set examples for how to stand up to hate. But they also represented parables, precedents of what we could expect if we protested our removal. Each one was convicted for defying the president's orders and sent to jail.

Unlike them, I never really had the option of civil disobedience. I was a child, and I wasn't going to hire a lawyer. Like most 9-year-olds, I followed the path my parents carved for me. Eventually, I had to visit that language-school-turned-office for inoculations. The employees were obsessed with disease, and they insisted that illness wasn't an option, I suppose because the optics of a mass pandemic in a closed-off camp look a lot like genocide. And so before we went anywhere, we had to go through a series of vaccines, until officials felt sure we wouldn't all wind up dead.

Then, we were off.

Pomona

The guards searched us. Our bodies became potential hiding places for weapons as they looked for a stray knife or camera. To them, both objects were a present and immediate danger.

The weapons made sense; no guards wanted their guns to be rivaled on a long train ride. But the reason for a ban on cameras was less clear. Of course, the government had detained us in the first place out of fear we might commit espionage, so logically, they may have been worried that we would take sensitive photos if we had access to cameras. But that would have only mattered if we were free. By the time we were being loaded onto buses, we had no way to get footage to the Japanese government, even if we had wanted to — which no one did.

It's more likely that federal officials didn't want a record of what happened to us. They didn't want Japanese-Americans documenting the treatment they faced, because if there was no visual proof, very few people would believe them. A picture is worth a thousand words, and in a country where we tended to assume the best about our elected officials in the 1940s, claims of abuse while unlawfully incarcerated were unlikely to get anyone's attention (especially when those making such claims did not have white skin).

But if there were photos, U.S. citizens would not have been able to look away. Photos of guards pointing guns at children. Photos of crowded mess halls, inedible food, and bathroom lines out the door. Photos of a family of four cramped into living quarters meant for a horse. No, no one could have looked away from those. And I would imagine that's why the guards searched us for cameras.

After we were inspected in San Francisco, we boarded a bus to Pomona, California, on May 12, 1942, where for three months we stayed at a race track they shut down to hold us during the war. We replaced the horses as livestock as we packed into smelly stables or tiny shacks, waiting for freedom. The government called these places assembly centers, but they were really temporary prisons because they were surrounded by fences and armed guards in watch towers. Plus, once we assembled, we could not disperse.

There were 5,514 of us. 5,514 souls stuck into 300 barracks built on a race track parking lot. Wants were not a concern; we could not even get what we needed. There were eight bathrooms and as many mess halls between all of us, which meant 700 people relied on one set of toilets and a single dining facility.

I remember the lines. Every day was a series of long lines, waiting for the opportunity to go to the bathroom or fill our stomachs with food that for us was nearly inedible. I don't recall eating much in Pomona. What they served us was too repugnant to swallow.

But it was better to be outside in a line than trapped in our room. "Room" is really too pleasant of a word; these were shacks, all huddled together in a row with a thin layer of plywood barely dividing one family from the other. The walls did not reach the ceiling, and as a child, I fell asleep to the sounds of other people's anguish. Tucked in an unbreathable room with four cots— one each for me, Nob, Mom and Dad—we could not walk, or move, or live. We just had to listen.

I heard the cries of a young boy screaming his head off and wondered if he was being tortured. His mother was giving him his first enema. I heard neighbors sobbing, coughing, shouting. I heard the familiar echoes of grief far more often than those of joy, and I could not block them out. That was the soundscape of Pomona, orchestrated by General DeWitt, a maestro of suffering. I felt I had been mistakenly committed to a madhouse, my ears burdened by the strange dissonances of pain and desperation.

I could not escape the room, either. Once we were settled in for the night, all I could see was four walls closing in on me. Telling me I was trapped. It was summer, and as other kids played in the sun, I had been condemned to prison. No one had told me my crime, nor my sentence. I would reside in this room until I didn't, and no one I trusted could tell me when that would be.

As the months ticked by, we found ways to entertain ourselves. We gave into the spectacle. Those of us who were already behind the gate watched in crowds as the next load of Japanese Americans were brought to our stables. After we were detained and under close surveillance, some of us were allowed to get cameras, and I have a photograph from those days. We witnessed our race being rounded up and quarantined, and all we could do was look on. We could not save anyone when we couldn't even save ourselves.

And so Pomona was the worst. It was a purgatory that looked more like hell than heaven. A land of waiting and wishing for change — any kind. A world where we were animals and treated with perhaps less respect than the prize mares that came before us at this racetrack. 5,514 of us were a collective nobody, exiled to a collective nowhere. We could hear each other's cries, but outside, no one was listening.

Parents forced to register families, Courtesy of the National Archives/ Dorothea Lange

The Dentist

My mother could have been shot in Pomona.

We all could have been shot. The guards who stood shoulder to shoulder blocking us into the race track parking lot could have fired on any of us. But my Okaasan made the fatal mistake of forgetting her shackles, and so she came closer to death than most.

We were visiting a dentist. I had developed a toothache, and at Pomona, the government had agreed that children could go into a nearby town for dental care as long as they were accompanied by a parent and armed guard. We played by the rules so I could get the attention I sorely needed, and my mother and I found our way to a dentist's office with a boy and his gun escorting us.

But the young guard made a mistake—it was his fault. While I was in the dentist's chair, he abandoned his post.

"Don't leave this office," he told my mother, and she understood him. But perhaps her maternal instincts kicked in, or perhaps the full weight of imprisonment had not yet collapsed on her. Perhaps she even thought she might outpace the guard, who was running errands of his own.

Either way, my mother dared to do something she had done a million times before, when she had self-sovereignty. She dared to go to the drug store.

When the guard returned, my Okaasan was still gone. He was frantic. He demanded to know where my mother was—as though she might abandon her youngest son in a dentist's chair to run away from our government—and when she came back with her bag of necessary shopping, he screamed at her in the middle of the dentist's office.

He would be in trouble, he said. What was she thinking, he said. He was there to watch us, he said.

My mother kept apologizing. She had not meant to do anything wrong, she said. She needed something from the store, she said. She thought it would be okay, she said. She was just living, as she had always been taught to live in America. Freely.

It was embarrassing, to have my mother screeched at by a barely-adult in uniform, his big weapon clutched tight to emphasize his only claim to power. But we were lucky his temperament did not predispose him to excessive violence, as others in law enforcement uniforms have been known to perpetrate. My mother got a tongue-lashing. She could have gotten a bullet.

And so this young guard drove home a larger reality for my 9-year-old self. We now lived in a country where my mother could have died for going to the drug store. She could have been shot for buying a few essentials. Everyday chores now deserved capital punishment, but only if your skin wasn't pearly white and your hair wasn't blond.

We Japanese were not entitled to the same lives as our white peers. Our children could not even have a toothache without fearing that death might haunt a routine visit to the dentist. We were spies and traitors, even if some of us had never been to Japan. We were different, and we never wouldn't be again.

We were the enemy. And thanks to us, the guard got to be a hero.

The Train

In Pomona, our travels weren't over — not even close. We had been stuck in a corner of California while ten more permanent mass imprisonment camps were constructed around the country. And once the Heart Mountain camp was ready for us that August, we boarded a train.

The problem was, we weren't ready for Wyoming. No one had told us where we were going, and we had no warm clothes, no winter wear. When we settled into our train cars, we didn't know how long we would be traveling, or where we would land.

We were blind. As we gathered at the train station, armed guards surrounded us. Their rifles warned that if we tried to escape, they would shoot, and our blood would be the only part of us to run through the streets. Big, serious, and daunting, they would be our companions for the entire ride to Heart Mountain.

Prisoners lived in horse stables, Courtesy of the National Archives/Dorothea Lange

Much like the boy at the dentist, these guards were peculiar in their indifference. They herded us into trains as though we were no one, and as they condemned us to years in prison they neither smiled nor scowled. In fact, it seemed they had no feelings at all about what was being done to us. We were their charges, and they were doing their jobs.

Once we were corralled, we spent three days and three nights on that prisoner's train, even though the trip itself should only take about 16 hours. As time ticked by, we kept pulling over to let regular passenger trains pass; we were the anomaly, and they deserved their peace. We would wait.

I was one of the lucky ones. In Pomona, I had caught some illness, despite all the inoculations, so I was thrown in a Pullman car with beds where I could stretch out and get comfortable. Most people didn't have that luxury; they sat on stiff benches for 72 hours.

There were some creature comforts onboard — a dining car filled with delicious eats, mainly — but almost no one took advantage. The prices were too steep, and waiters complained that we didn't tip well. So instead, we ate boxed lunches filled with bland sandwiches, an American staple unfamiliar to the Japanese palate. That was okay, in a way. We had gotten used to it. Since we left San Francisco, there had been no Japanese food in sight, and we ate what we were given.

My mother spent the days with the rest of the family — Dad, Nob, and my grandparents. But at night, she curled up with me in the Pullman car. I guess she was lucky, too, lucky that her youngest son's illness afforded her a bed to sleep in.

Though most of the three days were spent in our seats, we did get some reprieve. When the train would screech to a stop, we could climb out for fresh air and a little walk. But we were never allowed to feel alone: Armed guards encircled us to make sure we didn't escape.

Courtesy of the National Archives/Clem Albers

Then again, how could we? Escape? We didn't even know where we were. It wasn't until we pulled into a Wyoming station that we met our new home.

After tumbling out of the train, we shuffled onto the backs of army trucks for a half-mile drive through the main prison gates and into the Heart Mountain camp. I just remember the wind, and the dust, even in August. As we rode through what would prove an abominable snow monster of a state a few months later, the wind blew us to and fro and the dust swirled around us. It may have been hot, but it still somehow felt dangerous, like even the weather would try to make us miserable as we navigated a vast, raw terrain that was completely foreign to us.

And then, all of a sudden, we were there. At Heart Mountain, we were shown to our assigned barracks and cells for the night, and we settled in again. Together, our entire family filled a room the size of a small college double. Admittedly, it was better than Pomona — not by much, but by enough. There was still no privacy, no room to be. Just space to survive. That should have terrified us. After Pomona, we knew the conditions under which the U.S. government was willing to hold American children for a few months. This more polished front should have suggested a red flag. We would not be here temporarily. This was not our holding place for a season. This was our new life, and it would last for what felt like forever.

People would leave us. We would lose things. Our lives would never be the same. As we stepped onto Heart Mountain's grounds for the first time, it should have been foreboding. Because we were dying.

The lives we had known were now over. We weren't Kiyoshi, or Nob, or any of the other innocent children we had been. We weren't people who did things. We were now people who things had done to them—things that would be permanent. Things that would never leave us. Things that would make us who we are.

And that's where the story truly begins.

Life and Death

You have to remember: We were prisoners. Tucked away in Wyoming's expanse, we were forgotten by the outside world. No one cared about what happened to us, and no one fought for justice. Either we were invisible, or the average American was blind. And either way, we were not only lost to history, but also to the present.

As I write about Heart Mountain, your stomach may not always toss and turn. Sometimes, you might be struck by the mundanity of it all, our particular reality that hinged on an act of normalcy. For three years, mass imprisonment was our daily lives, and to forge forward, we had to dig through the weeds to find a fragment of beauty, a semblance of living. And so when I tell you about how we learned, and grew, and played, and ate, you may see yourself in me and my family, and even some of our friends.

But never forget: You are free. We were in a cage, its parameters drawn by scraggly fences.

I was 9 years old when I arrived at Heart Mountain. I was 12 when I finally left. Every day in between, I traipsed through the same boring routine as an inmate for a crime I never committed, and would never commit. Because when it came down to it, I loved my country. I always would.

Heart Mountain, Wyoming prison camp,
Courtesy of the Heart Mountain, Wyoming Foundation

My schedule was monotonous, empty. The weekdays were the okay times, when studies occupied my hours. They weren't much except a distraction. Our grammar school was nothing to look at; some Wyoming locals threw a fit when they heard we were getting new educational facilities, and though the government finished building our high school, the primary schools never got off the ground because nearby residents thought prisoners didn't deserve shiny new institutions. Housed in barracks that were supposed to be living quarters, roomful after roomful of Japanese-American students like me learned what we could, considering.

At Heart Mountain, I went through much of middle school. I was a mediocre student, with mostly "Cs" on my report card. Applying myself seemed like a silly notion when nothing I did ever really mattered. We weren't going to get to leave, even if we did perform well, and it was so much easier to be defiant than to play along.

In school, we got the basics, just enough not to fall behind. In the meantime, we acted like delinquents — all of us. No one wanted to sit still from dawn to dusk studying in a sorry excuse for a school, so we behaved as badly as we could. Quiet and withdrawn, our teacher didn't really know how to control us, and as middle schoolers, we preyed on her weaknesses.

I still remember one morning, when she fumbled through the door without saying a single word. She would continue like that all day, mute. In complete silence, she sat there with indignation. Her point was clear: She wouldn't teach us anything if we wouldn't listen.

I guess the education at Heart Mountain was fine; modeled after the state's public school curriculum, we had to meet standards, even if we were working out of a shanty house. Like I said, the weekdays were always alright. It was the weekends when we got in trouble — the weekends when our brains swam with boredom, when there was nothing to do but sleep, and eat, and sleep again.

Our parents tried hard to change that. They were always organizing some activity to keep us occupied, so our imaginations wouldn't drift off to other, less productive places. At camp, there were no less than 12 Boy and Girl Scouts groups. Our leaders were prisoners, too — people who nevertheless taught us who America wanted us to be, even as it incarcerated us for who we were. Somehow, our moms and dads coughed up the money for real uniforms, like the ones on the outside, and so we were all dressed in our little hats and ties, spitting images of American patriots.

I myself was a Cub Scout and learned the fundamentals of that world. I tried to be organized, to follow the scout's pledge, and most of all, to be a good U.S. citizen.

Though we were almost completely an internal operation, sometimes, Scouts from the outside would visit. Future Senator Alan Simpson came when he was just a boy, and in the unlikeliest of circumstances, he made a new friend named Norman. Decades later, Congressman Mineta served as a U.S. representative for terms and terms, as well as the Secretary of Transportation in George W. Bush's cabinet. It was Alan who inspired Norman to seek political office in the first place.

As the children entertained themselves with American idealism, there were other ways for adults to pass the days. No one could teach Japanese — the U.S. government thought our language posed some kind of threat, and that if we learned it, we'd be more dangerous (unfortunately for them, most of us already spoke it, and collectively, we disproved their theory). But the same wasn't true of English, and the high school hosted ESL classes at night, where prisoners could learn to assimilate. For their part, my parents never went. My dad already spoke English fluently from college, and in the confines of an ethnic jail, Mom had no interest in picking up any more linguistic skill than she already had. That was fine. My brother and I were both bilingual, so we all got by.

34

There was a camp economy, too, an industry to keep our hands busy. Constantly, we threw weddings and funerals — more funerals than weddings. The hospital at Heart Mountain could treat ordinary ailments, but when someone contracted a more obscure disease, they were out of luck. Most of the bodies we buried were of the elderly, though of course there were a few kids. There always are, when neglect is the law of the land. People die too soon because they are never given a chance to live.

A woman from the camp floral society making flower arrangements for funerals using paper, Courtesy of the Heart Mountain Wyoming Foundation

Every month, three or four new corpses would need a memorial, so we averaged about a service per week. At funerals, just like at weddings, you need flowers. In Wyoming, we didn't have too many blooming buds, especially during the winter, so all the women came together to start their own flower-making groups. Out of paper, they folded delicate blossoms to adorn lapels or halls or lay on caskets or graves, depending on the occasion.

The adults also started their own gardens. In the mess hall, meals of mushy, canned produce turned our stomachs, and so even as kids, we wouldn't eat much. This wasn't the food we knew from back home, where we ate lean proteins and fresh vegetables. So our parents decided to harvest their own legumes at the camp, coaxing out of a bitter earth something that was actually edible.

I remember one day, about two years into our detention. My mother was convinced she would make us a home-cooked pie like the ones we had in San Francisco. Pumpkin. Apple. She wanted to give us a taste that wasn't generic or burdened by resentment. She wanted to give us a piece of what we left behind, and by doing so, let us reclaim who we were before we became no one.

Deliberate, almost foolhardy, my mother stripped hanger wire into a semblance of a pan rack. Instead of the fresh, juicy fruit we knew from home, she must have used canned produce preserved in perfect mediocrity for years — it was all she could access, and perhaps she thought we would not know the difference after it was baked in a pie. She set her makeshift pan rack and her makeshift pie on the upper level of our coal burning stove and waited. She willed it to work. It was her one chance to feign normalcy, to feel in control of something as maternal as baking a pie.

When she opened the stove to check on her creation, the hanger wire had melted from overwhelming heat. The pie had fallen off its now decayed pedestal to become ash, and her hopes burned with it. It has been seven decades since that moment, and yet the clarity remains — how my mother was broken, and all by a pie.

Sometimes, we bought things, if we could afford them. Things like clothes. In Wyoming's chill, we needed more padding than what we were used to in San Francisco. That first winter got down to negative 28 degrees, and for children who had never seen snow, the wind chill was completely foreign. The military issued us some of its gear — adult-sized outerwear that worked well for our parents, but flooded over us like we were playing dress up. The government stuffed me in a Navy pea coat that completely drowned me in fabric, until my parents took to the Sears catalogue and ordered something in a child's size. That's how most of the adults did it — they paid big bucks for halfway decent services that brought packages all the way out to camp. And so we all ended up looking like we had uniforms anyway, because we were all wearing the exact same styles from Sears. They were our only options. Individuality would have to wait.

Personally, my family usually couldn't buy too much — General DeWitt froze all the bank accounts that belonged to Japanese names, and my father relied on his white friends from back home to send us clothes and other essentials. It wasn't easy, to pretend like our charity and scarcity were normal. But eventually, it just became a fact of life.

To be less reliant, we tried to scrimp. My mother ordered us sizes that would last for years as our bodies grew and changed because we could not afford the luxury of newness every season. I remember the pair of snow boots she got me; they swallowed my feet whole. I looked like clowns who stumble over themselves, one foot tripping the other in a constant loop of clumsiness and embarrassment. And I was embarrassed. I may have been the class jokester back in San Francisco, but I had no intention of becoming a clown — especially not in a place where nothing felt funny.

I never noticed the other kids' shoes. Maybe they gaped wide like mine, exposing with every millimeter the frugality of a family. Or maybe others could afford new shoes every time they grew a size. It never occurred to me to see whether the rest of the children could empathize; I was too mortified. I just wanted to hide.

It should have been a sign that none of the kids teased me. Middle schoolers can be cruel; the skill is an inherent gift bestowed upon them by countless hormones raging inside that want to be let out. Those hormones are only exacerbated by the angst of feeling trapped for no apparent reason. But the other kids never picked on me for my big shoes — something they could have noticed so easily, were such scarcities not normal to them. In camp, there were not poor kids or rich kids, or even middle class kids. There were just kids who had had their lives stolen from them, and who now existed in limbo.

Despite everything, life went on in camp, as it tends to do until it doesn't. There were babies — 558 of them.

Newborns. In a place where families were all shoved into a single cell with no breathing room, I still wonder at how anyone found the privacy to conceive and give birth. But they did, again and again. At least 558 times. And for those infants, life in camp was the status quo — a status quo that ravaged the status quo living inside the people who could still remember life before Pearl Harbor.

Though we tried to feign normalcy, our home lives were falling apart. In barracks of hundreds, we forgot how to be a nuclear family. Our parents watched as we gravitated toward friends instead of them. When we should have been sitting with our loved ones in the mess hall, we chose to join cliques. Whereas we used to eat dinner as a family, now, we were a house divided.

Signs along the perimeter fence warned Japanese Americans not to cross the fence,
Courtesy of Heart Mountain Wyoming Foundation

It didn't matter that our parents had worked tirelessly to try to give us a decent life behind barbed wire fences. We were stuck, and they couldn't make us unstuck. We couldn't return to our dining room tables in San Francisco, and we couldn't eat poultry, and whole milk, and an occasional hamburger when we wanted. We no longer held our fates in our hands, and our parents couldn't fix that. They couldn't stop our imprisonment. They couldn't choose to fight it, in a place where no one could hear us. Only the president, or Congress, or the courts could decide whether to end our suffering, and as Americans fought Japanese soldiers in the Pacific, they wouldn't dare.

And so the days dragged on for three years. People were lost, people we loved. People changed, and people learned a new normal. Often, people felt less like people, and more like hostages. People disappeared into the heart of Wyoming, and other people didn't seem to care.

That's why you have to remember: We were prisoners. Signs along the camp's perimeter were always there to remind us of that.

They spoke of danger and retribution should we ever try to cross the fences and be free. "Evacuees," they read, "Stay 10 Feet Away From Fence."

Part 2: Getting By

How Do I Feel?

I couldn't walk. At 10 years old, I learned that pain could make me bedridden, siphoned off from my family and friends at camp. On an island of misfits, I spent my days with a few other boys whose ailments went beyond broken bones and common colds as we waited to miraculously heal, or else waste away until we were nothing.

The boredom lasted for hours, day after day. In a hospital ward that was more decorated but no less cramped than our barracks, we lay in three or four beds only feet from each other. We sat there with no entertainment, nothing but the hurt each of us felt for reasons we could not understand. Our lack of knowledge stemmed mainly from our doctors, who took days to diagnose us and still never seemed to arrive at the right conclusion.

For me, they came up with arthritis. Arthritis of the muscle, to be exact. Decades later, I would sift through the National Archives to discover that these physicians did not even know basic anatomy — arthritis occurs in joints, not muscles. And my joints felt fine; it was the muscle that kept me in bed.

But in the end, their diagnosis didn't matter. Not really. Because their treatment was so basic that it left little room for either error or progress.

All I remember is hot packs, so many compresses smooshed against the sharp pain in my leg. They never even soothed the problem. I couldn't walk, couldn't leave the hospital. For weeks, I was tucked inside a ward, a ghost to the outside world, with no remedy in sight. And those hot compresses were still handed to me day after day, night after night, as I wallowed alone. The doctors seemed to believe the useless packs were my only hope.

It was my mother who had sent me off to the camp hospital in an ambulance after she found me struggling, and my parents came to see me every once in a while. They were my only visitors, the only people who relieved me from the ward's weary doldrums. My other companions belonged to my medical dystopia, where everyone was either sick or sick of caring.

Most of the words I spoke were to a nurse. "How do you feel?" she would ask. And usually, I didn't feel any different. My leg still wouldn't work properly, and I was still a captive of a hospital inside an internment camp, two separate kinds of jails.

Sometimes, the other kids would pipe in, too. Most of them were fine, but there was another boy who hated the place as much as I did. Once, while I was sleeping, he found a pair of scissors and chopped off my hair. He picked fights with me to pass the time, and his tantrums annoyed me. None of us wanted to be there. But making scenes wouldn't help the hours go by faster; it would just mean conflict when our lives were already filled with enough drama.

Then again, I wasn't exactly a model patient, either. One evening, I covered my bed like I was sleeping and dressed myself in a bathrobe. With the night blanketing the sky, I thought I could escape to my barrack, and my cell, and my cot. But the nurse caught me, and she sent me back to the ward. I didn't have the right to be discharged. I couldn't refuse medical treatment. I couldn't even go back home, not to San Francisco, but just down a few paces to be with my family. I was a captive who couldn't opt out of "help," even when it wasn't helping. My health — my voice — had no importance.

Weeks later, I was discharged from the hospital. My leg miraculously healed, no thanks to hot compresses or false diagnoses, and once I could walk on my own, I rejoined the camp's delicate normalcy. But I never forgot being stuck in a hospital, where the doctors couldn't tell me what was wrong, and where I lay in agony wondering what would happen to me. Would I ever walk? Would I ever play? Would I ever be able to shatter this illusion of living in Wyoming and rejoin a world I once knew, or was this my new reality, tied to a bed even if I returned home to San Francisco?

And then, there was always that nagging question. One that tugs at me more today than it did back then.

Could the doctors in California have done something to cure me?

But if I'm being honest, that question doesn't apply so much to me. Not really. I got better. Without medicine, without treatment, I got up and pushed on. I lived.

That question is for all the people who weren't so lucky.

Shortchanged

My grandfather made miso. Tsunegoro Mihara sailed across an ocean in 1902 to arrive on California shores. For 18 years before my father and grandmother followed, soybean paste was his life. It was what he could sell, and each vat represented opportunity for my dad back in Japan. And so Tsunegoro made batch after batch for San Franciscans, who in turn would use the miso for a Japanese delicacy. All at once, he lived between two locations: Geographically, he was in America, but professionally, he always inhabited Japan. And personally, he waited for the people he loved to join him, so at least in one aspect of his life, he did not have to split himself between two ends of the Pacific.

Tsunegoro's wish was finally granted when my father graduated from a prestigious school and was offered the newsperson position in San Francisco. Suddenly, they were all together again, living under one roof. Even after Nob and I were born, my grandparents stayed with us in Japantown. It was a luxury, to live as one, undivided by bodies of water or continents.

I mostly remember my grandfather in the garden. Nob and I would watch him as he cared for the flora in our backyard. He was so careful, so masterful, that wealthy homeowners would invite him to curate their gardens, too. He fostered life — let it grow — and he tamed it to be beautiful.

Tsunegoro Mihara looking over his Bonsai garden,
Courtesy of the Mihara Family Collection

Tsunegoro had a special love of Bonsai trees. The goal was to shape the limbs just right so they jutted symmetrical, or slightly asymmetrical. With grandfather, they were mainly asymmetrical; his skill set pointed them that way. In grocery stores nowadays, pre-trimmed Bonsai trees may seem easy and instant. But back then, when not everything was automated or produced by mass labor, the Japanese technique represented a high art, a dignified capacity. And so my grandfather was an artist, calling on his culture and his eye to make a miniature representation of reality. His Bonsai trees were imperfect in their asymmetry, and yet astonishing as a model of life.

Tsunegoro was already nearing his 70s when Japanese forces attacked Pearl Harbor. But when we were all imprisoned, there was no differentiation between the young and old, the healthy and sick. He was escorted to a train just like us, and when we arrived at Heart Mountain, he and Grandmother were assigned to a barrack across the camp from ours. Together, they lived in a little apartment until May 5, 1944. Then, they would never live together again.

That was the night my grandfather went to the hospital. They never let him leave. For months, he lay in a bed as his body reduced to bare bones. When I was growing up in San Francisco, he always looked sturdy and healthy like me and my father. But the longer he languished in the camp hospital, the more gaunt and ghoulish he became. When I look at photos of the Holocaust today, I see my grandfather in those victims clinging to life, whose insides jut out of their flesh in unnatural, evil indentations. That was Tsunegoro. That was my grandfather as he became someone I no longer recognized.

The doctors at camp diagnosed him with colon cancer, but that wouldn't be what killed him. Instead, I believe it was the laxatives they shoved down his throat as "treatment" without any intravenous nutrition to nourish him. That milky medicine starved him to death until he was barely a person and almost a corpse. Those doctors killed him. The camp and the government neglected him and let him suffer. And I had to watch.

I visited him every few days, about twice a week. A lot of people did; he was a popular man. He would always ask us for food. He especially hankered for watermelon, and we brought him what we could, when we could. Still, it was odd that he wanted provisions from the mess hall when he sat in a hospital filled with food, where a meal shouldn't have been hard to come by. But he was always hungry, always starving, and perhaps we should have realized back then that his life was in danger. Of course, we knew the cancer could eat him alive. But we didn't know that what was meant to keep the disease at bay was actually devouring him from the inside.

Eventually, I got to the point where I didn't want to see him. He was so unsightly, such a remnant of himself. When someone is really sick, they get to a point where they've already become their ghost. And I hated seeing my grandfather's ghost as he sat there, trying to press on just a little longer in this life.

During that final moment when he was still coherent but knew he would die, Tsunegoro asked to see me, to say goodbye. I didn't want to go, but I knew I needed to, though it would be one of the worst experiences of my young life. And so at 11 years old, I held communion with a man just before he vanished into the cosmos.

"Come close," Tsunegoro whispered, and I did. He slipped a quarter into my palm. "I don't have much money left, but I want you to have this," he said. "Be my guest, take care of yourself."

I remember those four words so distinctly: "Take care of yourself." In his last moments, my grandfather was thinking about me, about his family. And that made sense. He had devoted his life to us; why would he not give us his death as well?

On August 6, 1944, Tsunegoro passed away in camp, in a hospital, a double captive. He was 72 years old.

Tsunegoro Mihara with a miso making machine,
Courtesy of the Mihara Family Collection

But the story continues. It always does. Death is a false and fickle marker of the end, because there are always the people who get left behind. And this time, the person left behind was my grandmother. After her husband died, she had to figure out the logistics of death inside a prison. She could not escort his body back to San Francisco; the U.S. government was so afraid of Japanese residents that it even barred our lifeless corpses and their wives from returning home. We were a threat, even if we couldn't breathe, or move, or speak. Even if death's cloak had already wrapped us in an unending slumber.

There was a cemetery at camp, but my grandmother had no intention of sentencing her husband to eternal damnation at Heart Mountain. We would leave, of that she felt certain. And he would come with us. No one deserved to be stuck in prison for the rest of forever, and especially not someone she loved.

And so she had one choice, which when you think about it, isn't really a choice at all. Tsunegoro would be cremated. His ashes would sit in Grandmother's apartment until she could finally return to San Francisco and spread them along the family plot, where he would belong.

Tsunegoro's funeral at a prison barrack, Courtesy of the Mihara Family Collection

But in 1944 there were no crematories in all of Wyoming, and so Tsunegoro would have to take a trip. Loaded into a shipping container on a freight train, his remains traveled all the way to Montana, into a fiery furnace, and then back into Grandmother's arms.

Before he went, we held a funeral inside the barracks. There were crowds of people there, and so many paper flowers. Grandfather had been beloved, that much was clear.

The adults opted against an open casket. Tsunegoro looked too ill, too vacuous to fill the shoes of a man we had all known. It was better not to look and instead to remember him as he once was. As he had always been. As he would always be.

I remember attending the funeral. There were other young people there, and I phased in and out of mourning and play like an 11-year-old does. In a photo from that day, I still look like a child, though I'm dressed like an adult. In a white shirt, tie, and jacket, I'm nestled between my grandmother in her veil and my father in his suit. My face is twisted at an angle that says, "I'm heartbroken but won't admit it, because I'm an 11-year-old boy, and I'm stuck in prison, and now my grandfather is gone forever." It says, "Even if I get to go home one day, I'll have lost something — someone — that I can never get back."

It says, "After today, my life will never be the same. And right now, I don't know how to deal with that."

Blind, Part 2

Our family arrived at Heart Mountain on August 25, 1942. Just under a year later, my father was diagnosed with chronic glaucoma. And by May of 1945, he was already blind.

At least, that's the story my dad's medical record tells. But like all things at camp, the reality was much more nuanced than a few sentences could ever say.

My father came to Heart Mountain with glaucoma; his eyes were failing him back in 1942, but he had learned how to tame them. He knew he would eventually have to strain in order to make out what lay in the distance. He knew his clarity would blur and his vision wane. But he had no idea that within a few months' time, he would struggle to read words he had once written, and that within a few years, he would not be able to see at all.

A pair of spectacles represented his journey. Back in San Francisco, he didn't need lenses. But after a few months in Wyoming, he started wearing these thick glasses to help him manage. That was not especially telling — people wear glasses for much of their life, like any other piece of clothing. It's necessary, but it's also not a handicap. It just is.

What was telling was when he took the glasses off, and never put them back on. That meant they didn't help anymore. That meant he had given up on them.

My father's medical record shows that the doctors at camp knew what was happening to him. Difficulty seeing became a recommendation to stop working, which then devolved into a significant decrease in visual power. Eventually, that gave way to total blindness in the right eye.

The progression was clear, its end result obvious and imminent.

But if the doctors could identify the problem, they couldn't fix it.

Like when my grandfather and I were in the hospital, there were no specialists to opine on more clinically complicated issues. The staff could not offer drops, or prescriptions, or surgeries that might de-cloud the mist that was permanently invading his pupils. They could only listen, and write notes, and introduce them into his file without providing a solution — or even a plan of action.

Of course, the change didn't happen overnight. It was a progression, a drawn-out descent that my father had to witness, and feel, and relay. It was a downward spiral into darkness, a gradual lowering into a cave where like in Plato's Republic, all that was left by the end were dancing shadows. My father who had loved reading words on a page had to slowly realize that no matter how large the print, he would never engage with a text in the same way again.

For our family, that had a larger meaning. Without his vision, my Otoosan would never find employment at a paper again. As workers, one of the qualifications we take for granted is our basic sense of sight — until we lose it. And my father lost it. Once we left camp, we knew he would have no vocation, no way to provide for us like he had before the war. He would no longer be a high-powered journalist, because soon, he would be blind.

And it was the government's fault. Back in San Francisco, my dad had found a qualified ophthalmologist who could treat his illness. The glaucoma was under control. But when he came to camp and his condition grew worse day by day, Lieutenant General DeWitt denied him the right to visit his doctor in California. He was going blind, but he was still a defense risk. Even though the Japanese forces would never choose someone who couldn't see to spy for them. Even though he couldn't do his own job anymore, much less contribute to a more engaged, clandestine operation. In the minds of the government, sending him to San Francisco could mean a breach in security, just by going to an ophthalmologist's office that might save his sight.

By late-October of 1944, my father knew he was in trouble. He asked to see another ophthalmologist near camp, someone who could at least provide relevant advice and maybe even offer relief. By then, we had been in camp for more than two years. We were broke, living off $19 a month of disability payments, and my dad asked for government aid for the visit. A few days later, a camp physician wrote in his record that he was completely blind in one eye and nearly blind in the other. And so the doctor recommended my father see a specialist.

That was the window. That was the moment to do something — anything. But instead, the government did nothing, and my father just waited.

There were no glaucoma specialists in Wyoming. Dad would have to go to Montana, where he was finally sent to a hospital in Billings on May 31, 1945 — six months after the initial recommendation. When he got there, the doctor said it was too late. His eyesight was rapidly deteriorating, and no medication or surgery could salvage even a remnant of it. He was told to return to camp and rest, a blanket statement that meant there was nothing left to do. His vision was gone.

Basically, it was as if the government had sent a man to see a cardiovascular specialist, after a heart attack had already struck him dead.

For years, I felt a deep bitterness about how officials treated my father — how they let his sight become a casualty of Heart Mountain, yet another death in the family. But for his part, my dad never let his illness defeat him. He always stayed busy, always fought to be a productive member of society even when his body pushed him to shrink and cower from the world. He wrote books. With the help of a craftsman, he devised his own system of Japanese braille that was eventually disseminated in Japan and deployed widely. Each symbol etched into wood related to a Japanese character, and with it, my father continued to learn, and communicate, and create in his native language. Even during one of his most trying moments, he chose to be a pioneer rather than a martyr.

If Dad ever became depressed, he never showed it. He was an innovator, and even as the world closed in, he would open doors for others like him.

In the darkest days, my father was never completely blind. He could still see ways to make the world a better place, and for him, for a while, that was good enough. He couldn't prevent his illness. But he could keep it from defining him.

And so Tokinobu Mihara became the living manifestation of perseverance at Heart Mountain. His medical record may have told one story. His life told another.

Braille Board, Courtesy of Mihara Family Collection

Hope

Sometimes, life is magical. The first time we feel love from someone who didn't have to give it to us. Our first taste of success. The first time we read something that touches us. Our first words where we feel truly understood.

Even at a place as hollow as Heart Mountain, magic lurks in the wind, and the clouds, and the grass, and the open skies. And I found my magic sitting on the steps to my cell, waiting for something good to happen after years stuck in a camp.

It was a plane. Probably a commercial plane; there was no need for the U.S. Air Force to police us when we didn't even stand a chance against the guards. Maybe it carried mail — well wishes from every corner of the world, taking short trips from airfield to airfield.

There was nothing special about this plane. It would have meant nothing if I hadn't been sitting there, hoping for a miracle. But I was. And I looked up. And it was mine.

In all its modest majesty, this small aircraft zoomed past to tell me something. It whispered the word freedom, and I heard it loud and clear. The plane represented what I could not have, what I wanted most in the world. What I coveted. Anyone with a plane could never be trapped in a place like Heart Mountain. It was the ultimate agency, the most unwavering promise of emancipation.

Of course, birds were like that, too. But humans could not become birds. When I saw birds in Wyoming, their wings were not an attainable goal. If they had been, we would have all become birds; giving up our personhood would have been a small price to pay.

But unlike wings, an airplane I could make. People owned airplanes. People flew airplanes. People designed airplanes. Airplanes were the wings humanity gave to himself so that no one could enslave him. They were the promise of other horizons — whichever horizons you wanted to see. They were a ride a thousand miles away, and they could rescue you if they were yours.

Of course, planes are also ephemeral. They're here, and then they're gone. Unless they're yours, they do not care about you. Except this one did. This one stayed. This one never left me; it lived inside my mind as a reminder of who I would become.

That plane shaped the rest of my life. It gave me a purpose. It motivated me to wait, to get through what felt like eternal damnation and then never depreciate my life again. It told me what I wanted. I wanted to be an engineer, so that people would have ways to be free. People like me. Maybe I would save us.

But first, I had to escape Heart Mountain. And hope could not even help me fly away.

Part 3: Getting Out

Escape?

It was a game. The guards were cats. We were mice. But this time, we were the ones who had nine lives. And for a chance to feel free, we put all of them on the line.

Back then, we didn't know what was at stake. Not really. We didn't know that the guards had shooting orders if they saw anyone try to leave, or that their trigger-happy reflexes had already killed our counterparts at other camps — several Japanese Americans who were shot when they weren't even trying to escape. We didn't know that our shenanigans could end with a bullet in our backs, a pile of child corpses in the heart of Wyoming. We didn't know that the game we played wasn't just a game, but instead a prison break, with all the consequences that entailed.

All we knew was that we liked the adrenaline, and we needed some way to break the rules.

And so we broke out.

At Heart Mountain, watchtowers loomed over the camp so guards could keep an eye on their wards. The U.S. government somehow thought a bunch of Japanese-American civilians were brazen enough to require constant surveillance, and so guns pointed at us from above, like giants prepared to drown ants should they bite.

A boy tries to climb out of his prison camp, Courtesy of the Bill Manbo Collection

So for the most part, we didn't bite. But we did nibble sometimes.

At some point, we realized that guards were always on watch, but they weren't always watching. In those minutes when their minds wandered, bored of babysitting a camp where nothing and no one mattered, a handful of us would sneak up to the barbed wire fence and climb past.

We never went far. There wasn't really anywhere to go, except a river, where we would play games and mess with wildlife. We collected scorpions and lizards, and we had a running competition to see who could cut off the most rattlesnake tails. We let out our pent up anger by slicing snakes to bits, remnants of themselves. And we got good at it — I don't remember a single boy with a snake bite, but I do remember a lot of rattles.

We also collected found objects, things like arrowheads. Another testament to ferocity. We were transfixed by these weapons that Native Americans had left behind, and in some ways, that made sense. First of all, there are no arrowheads in San Francisco. This was new terrain, and we were exploring it. The opportunity for discovery was one of the few forces that could allow us to wander beyond the confines of ourselves — beyond the camp's walls and into a world of imagination where everything felt new and meaningful, if for only a moment.

But these arrowheads were also homages to the region's past, and to our present. The people who lived here before us had been brutalized by the power of the United States. So had we. And arrowheads were the tools they used to fight back. We never got to fight, but we did get to collect arrowheads. That was the closest we came to something that looked like the war that we waged inside ourselves — the war that told us our own government hated us, and that it was our moral duty to rebel.

By the river, there were moments of tenderness, too, when violence became care along the threshold of revelation. One day, we used slingshots to catapult rocks at nests. We thought they were empty. But then one fell, with a baby magpie tucked inside. The bird was hurt, but not dead, and my friend took it in his arms for a trip back to camp. The magpie became his pet, a fellow victim of unnecessary hurt during an aimless war in the Pacific. If World War II had never happened, then the Japanese forces would have never bombed

Pearl Harbor. If they had never bombed Pearl Harbor, then we probably would have never been sent to Heart Mountain. And if we had never been sent to Heart Mountain, that magpie would have never fallen out of his tree.

That's how war is: A chain of actions and reactions, none of them good. I guess with one gesture of kindness, my friend decided he could reclaim some control over all the chaos, the flying bullets and the innocents caught in the crossfire. One magpie could break the cycle of murder and pain.

I probably would have kept a magpie if I could — or a scorpion, or some other pet to distract me. But Nob and I weren't allowed to collect anything that breathed, our parents said. Arrowheads were fine. Arrowheads couldn't bite or sting.

During our adventures, some kids found other ways than ripping apart snakes and shooting nests to take care of their angst. One of my friends got himself a girlfriend, and they would sneak off to look for a haystack or hiding place where they could test out what it meant to be in love. Some of us would follow and watch what they did when they thought they were alone. To us, their escapades were funny, and in some ways they were: In a place where eyes are always watching, why wouldn't they follow you everywhere? Even your friends can be spies. Their intention may not be malicious, but the outcome is the same.

At first, only children explored beyond the fence; our parents didn't dare. But after about a year, the guards left their watchtowers. Adult prisoners gathered food from the mess hall for a picnic, and we walked right through the main gate to get to the river. Hundreds of us. Entire barracks. The guards stared blankly at us as we left for our day trip.

By that time, they had realized that even if people "escape" Heart Mountain, they never truly escape. Technically, even us kids were able to break out of the internment camp, but we rarely went past the river. We were still captives of Wyoming, 400 miles from the nearest transportation hub back to California. Plus, anyone out there in the expanse knew exactly who we were. If we intended to escape in earnest, we would be reported as fugitives within minutes.

So sometimes, the guards let us out. They knew we had nowhere to go, because no one ever escaped Heart Mountain.

A Trip to Cody

Once the government realized we would never actually escape — that our faith in them was too strong to ever stage a rebellion, and that our homes were unreachable from an almost tundric corner of the States — we earned brief forays into culture, and noise, and life. I cannot remember exactly when officials started issuing passes to Cody, Wyoming. I only remember how carefully they rationed them, so we wouldn't flood into the little town and overwhelm its inhabitants.

I don't know why we were such a liability. All we did was walk.

Up and down the main street of Cody, 13 miles from camp, my father and I strolled during our afternoon away. By then, he was completely blind, and his eyes could not distinguish between shapes and letters as we wandered by storefronts. He tasked me, his son, with acting as a translator, and so after every few paces I stopped to read the signs in shop windows that could help him imagine the scene.

In those days, Cody served as a first beacon of civilization outside of barbed wire, an indication of what had happened to America because of yet another world war. It was our first real venture into society since being rounded up and sent to Heart Mountain, but as an experiment, it didn't have any legs. We did not know how Cody's residents had viewed Japanese Americans back in 1940, before Pearl Harbor. Our only experiences with racial difference in the United States were from living beside other residents in San

Francisco, who were a far cry from the people who ran mom and pop shops and loved their small town in northwest Wyoming.

But I suppose what pre-existed the war doesn't really matter. It's what I discovered during that affected me for the rest of my life.

The Cody residents were the same people who had demanded we not have new schools. They had fought for us to be placed in prisons, and they had made it clear they didn't want us anywhere near their neighborhoods. When I finally made it onto their turf, I learned why.

As we meandered through Cody, I read each and every window sign to my dad. Some of them were benign, or even practical. They enticed window shoppers by dangling what they could find if they only peeked through the front door — "shoes," "clothes," "restaurant." But from the luxuries of food and dress we were barred. In every third storefront sat a sign that read, "No Japs."

The little money we had was just as good as anyone else's, and in a capitalist society, you would have thought these shops would want our business. But along a row of Cody establishments, our appearance made us something less than customers.

Before Cody, I had never witnessed racial hatred. Not really. I suppose I had lived it; racism was what had inspired our imprisonment, which in turn had taught me why I didn't belong with ordinary Americans. But even in the internment camps, we were not treated like a plague that could threaten the world around us.

As I read the signs over and over, I could not understand. "No Japs?" But what about Japanese Americans? Though my father could not see, he could hear the struggle in my voice as I tried to find a reason to despise myself so much, and to throw out racial slurs at boys and girls who were just as American as any Cody resident. It was then that he gave me the talk — the one that every minority parent dreads but still knows must take place. He taught me about racial hatred, and why the people of Cody loathed me just because of the color of my skin.

Signs around Cody forbade Japanese Americans from entering shops, Courtesy of Lyn Stallings/Park County Archives

That was the single worst moment of my imprisonment. Over illness. Over death. Over mushy foods and small living quarters and poor education. Our taste of freedom quickly transformed into a lesson about how cruel humanity can be when we turn to our basest instincts, and how even a young Japanese-American boy and his blind father can seem a threat when paranoia and hysteria reign.

Of course, there were some shops that let us in: The pharmacy, for one. In those, we could peruse and shop, pretending we were welcome. Who knows if we actually were, or if the thousands of Japanese-American customers visiting Cody just proved too much of an opportunity to pass up for owners who didn't let racism dictate their selling strategies. In the end, it was probably just good business.

No Escape

My father passed the test. On February 24, 1943, he took an exam to prove two things: He didn't want to return to his motherland, and he was loyal to the United States.

He answered question after question, like a shelter dog begging for someone to own him. To belong to America, he had to show that he could fit, that any difference people perceived should not make them afraid. Unlike the United States' time-tested doctrine, he was guilty until proven innocent, and the burden of proof to demonstrate his unbending support for the American experiment was on him. After almost a year of being imprisoned. After being detained and shipped off, like a felon. He would only get out if he proved that he was the spitting image of a patriot while inside.

There was a verbal section, an interrogation of sorts. He excelled in that, too, and he was rewarded for it. Soon, he was told that he could leave camp and go anywhere he liked. That is, anywhere but home. California was still off limits to anyone of Japanese blood, and so we could choose to start over or stay stagnant in Heart Mountain's unending time warp.

For a while, we waited. Waited for the tide to turn. Waited for the world to wake up. But when change came, it was not the kind we had wanted. After Mitsuye Endo won her case in 1944 and Japanese Americans were allowed to return to the West, we heard stories about how much Californians hated us. They had gone so far as to write their hatred into laws. Japanese laborers could no longer work on farms. Signs posted in front of homes told the first weary travelers, "Do not stop here — keep moving." Racism against us was worse in 1944 than it had been in 1942, when we were first rounded up and sent away because of it.

And so our home was no longer our home. Our prison would never be, either. Left with nowhere to go, my parents decided to start over.

On June 28, 1945, Nob, Mom, Dad and I packed up our meager belongings and boarded a bus. We had a permanent pass to leave Heart Mountain, and in that moment, I doubted I'd ever return to Wyoming. We moved onward to a new life in Salt Lake City, where like so many before us, we hoped we would find salvation.

But we soon learned that the mountain states could also feel hate, and their people could make us feel it, too.

When we arrived in Utah, my father devised a business plan that he thought might catch on. Completely blind, he could no longer edit copy, but he could still love books, and parchment, and pens. Within a block of the Mormon temple, he established the Oriental Culture Book Company, where he sold Japan-related literature and reading, as well as stationery and other writing goods. He set up shop in the middle of Salt Lake City's small Japantown — today's Salt Palace — and I'm sure he expected many of his clients to be like us. But he also hoped that he might find a white clientele who was curious about cultures other than their own, and who could appreciate the beauty of our world.

He sorely miscalculated, and he paid a price. The business floundered. No one cared about Asia — our beliefs, or thoughts, or prayers. At a time when difference proved a problem instead of an asset, no one wondered about horizons beyond the sights and sounds of Salt Lake City. Ingrained in my father's business model was an optimism that the world wanted to be globalized, or at least somewhat connected. In the mid-1940s, that desire didn't exist.

Meanwhile, our home life was deteriorating again, even outside the confines of a concentration camp. We had settled in West Salt Lake City, in a low-income district where diversity was the law of the land. But diversity didn't mean inclusion, and people of different backgrounds clashed with words that were as sharp as daggers. Our neighbors treated us poorly, and sometimes, we would find racial slurs or worse graffitied on our rental house.

When my mother couldn't take it anymore, we moved yet again, this time into a small room not unlike our single cell at Heart Mountain. A block from Dad's store, we found a cheap hotel where we all crammed in together because at least there, we were an unknown customer stopping by for a time, safe from the resentment that comes with the threat of permanence.

The Mihara family in front of a store in Salt Lake City,
Courtesy of the Mihara Family Collection

By then, the Oriental Culture Book Company was completely failing. I went out on the road, to Colorado or other Utah towns. I tried to sell a few measly objects, just something to get by. But wherever my family and I went, almost no one wanted a piece of Asia so soon after the Pacific War.

The breaking point came when on one of our trips, we crashed and nearly totaled the car, one of our last high-priced possessions. After that, Mom couldn't handle our vagabond life anymore. It was time to go home.

We had heard horror stories about San Francisco just after our imprisonment ended, but a few years later, the situation was supposed to be less severe. Calmer. Japanese Americans still struggled to work as professionals; instead of claiming positions for which they were qualified, they were assigned to blue collar posts, if they got a job at all. But the overwhelming hatred had dissipated; a new antagonism had already captivated the American consciousness, and as citizens learned to despise the Reds and their traitorous spies, "Japs" were old news. And so it was safer now to return to California.

Then, of course, there was the simple truth: Our experiment in Salt Lake City had failed. We couldn't keep living on nothing, and we couldn't make something in Utah. The racism we had hoped to avoid by moving slightly east was still alive and well. That was our great epiphany — our existence in the United States would likely be marked by otherness no matter where we went, so we might as well go home.

Three years after World War II ended, we moved back to San Francisco. And things got better.

There were low points. When our coffers became especially depleted, Mom had to work as a maid for a rich white family. That was our rock bottom in California, one that would have never happened without the war.

But my father was always an architect of life, and soon, he redesigned and rebuilt ours. We returned to our old house from 1942. It was so big, and we had grown accustomed to small. To pay off our bills, Dad chose to rent out some of the space to others who could use it. The living room became a dentist's office. Friends and family moved into some of the bedrooms. Together, we coexisted as a collective of people trying to reinvent ourselves.

In a backroom, my dad set up a school. Blindness does not keep brilliant minds from sharing their knowledge, and he had quite a few eager students. When the conflict in the Pacific ended, American GIs brought back scores of war brides. These women wanted to learn English and become U.S. citizens, and my father was their liaison between their old world and a new one. As he quizzed them on the branches of government or tested their English, he ensured that they would have a happy life stateside, even when his own was still in shambles because of what the U.S. government did to us.

Family outside of the Mihara home,
Courtesy of the Mihara Family Collection

The Oriental Culture Book Company survived Salt Lake City, too. Out of our home, my father continued to pawn books and magazines for a more active client base, and with all of his entrepreneurship, we got by.

As our life transformed, so did I. No longer a "C" student, I learned to prioritize school because my parents created an environment where education was paramount. All the Japanese parents did. They had been burned by the system, and they knew that their children would need a higher education to succeed in a world that had been carefully taught to hate them.

As for us kids, we did not talk about Heart Mountain after we left. In school, we discussed our coursework or our ambitions — the things we liked, that made us normal. Sometimes, a few stray teens from Japantown would remember the finer points of our imprisonment; how cold it was, how ridiculous we looked in our bulky clothes. But no one ever muttered the word "injustice." Though we may have known it in our hearts, our minds told us that what we had been through was no big thing. We certainly had not yet connected our struggles to any larger legal issue, and we weren't clamoring for reprisal. We just wanted to make our parents proud and go to college, and that meant leaving any unresolved angst for another day.

And so the world kept on spinning after our imprisonment, but for so many of us, it would never be the same.

In the end, wherever we turned, the memory of Heart Mountain followed all of us. There was no escape.

Be Like You

To me, Fumio Saito represented success. He was everything I wanted for myself, and he knew it. So when he told me to follow his lead, I listened.

The Saitos were the spitting image of what I wished my family could be. They had survived imprisonment and somehow seemed no worse for the wear, a perfect nuclear family with no scars or resentment. From the outside, they were wealthy business owners. All three of their kids were destined not only for college, but for the best institutions across the country. They had their pick of school — there were no financial hurdles to climb, no pressures too great to stifle potential.

What I didn't know until much later was that the Saitos were only an illusion. Business was bad. Mr. Saito struggled to keep his oldest son in school. Setsuko, Fumio's sister, had to take a low-paying job to help the household remain afloat.

But from where I stood, no one would have known. They seemed glamorous, whole. Untethered from the legacy of oppression. And I longed for that.

Though we were all interned together, I didn't really know the Saitos until I was in high school back in San Francisco. The family's youngest son Hiroshi was one of my closest friends, and I got to know his older brother Fumio during vacations, when he came home from the Massachusetts Institute of Technology. Fumio talked about his time at MIT — how all the professors were well-educated and his classmates brilliant. How he was learning so many things and felt challenged. How his social life flourished, even as he managed some of the hardest courses in the world.

His life sounded perfect, and I bought into what may have been real but was more likely a mirage. Fumio Saito became my idol, the person who willed me to achieve. He was the phantom for my own ambitions, filling the space that was once content being mediocre with a hunger for more. I did not want to become the "me" from before camp; that version of myself had been gone for a while now. Instead, I wanted to become Fumio Saito.

When Hiroshi transferred to Lick-Wilmerding High School his freshman year, I followed suit. After all, that's what the Saitos did, and I desperately wanted to be a Saito. Lick-Wilmerding High School is a small college preparatory school in San Francisco; when I was there, only about 500 students attended. I met with administrators to show them my report card filled with "B"s and all of a sudden, I was onboard. In classes with 20 students and lots of personalized attention, my "B"s suddenly became straight "A"s, and my dreams zoomed closer and closer so I could almost grasp them.

Meanwhile, as Fumio and I became friends, I confessed to him that I wanted to build planes. I had always known that there was a connection between aircraft design and engineering, but I didn't know what it was. He was the one who illuminated the field for me as he described his courses and I saw their inextricable link to that commercial airplane over Heart Mountain. When I was around 14 years old, Fumio told me that if I wanted to build rockets or aircrafts, I had to go to MIT. So that became my new goal, and I was sure I would reach it.

Fumio Saito was my role model. And so I would become just like him. Except I wasn't him, and as he delineated a path for me, I could never follow.

Ripples

In our lives, there are events that may seem isolated. But they never are. Lives are like children's building blocks slowly stacked upon one another. When one block is misplaced and begins to waver, the foundation becomes weaker. The tower tilts, ever so slightly, never to have the strength and stability it could have had if that single block had not gone amiss.

And my life was that way, too. As hard as I tried to fortify my tower, three years of childhood imprisonment made everything else shaky and unsure. I did not tumble or fall; I would not let myself. But sometimes, the world around me did wobble.

When I got into MIT, I thought I was on a path. It was everything I had wanted. I would be Fumio — maybe even better. I too would escape the legacy of oppression, and all would be well. I would build the planes that would free people, and I would never have to worry about being trapped again.

I told my father I had been accepted to the best engineering school in the country, with a scholarship. I thought he would be proud. Instead, he told me I couldn't go. He was blind. We were barely scraping by. The $3,000 a year for tuition and board would handicap us, and nothing else mattered. My scholarship didn't matter. My ambitions didn't matter. Regardless of what I said or did, I would not go to MIT.

I was devastated. In hindsight, I should have had more sympathy for my father — he was doing everything he could. It was the government's fault that we could not afford MIT; the government had not treated his illness before it was too late, and the government had made it to where my father could not provide opportunity for his children. The government had taken three years of our lives when we could have saved and prepared for college. And as hard as my father tried, he could not make up for the harms the government inflicted upon us.

At the time, when I learned my future was still being upset by Heart Mountain, the blow was crippling, and it was difficult to see the bigger picture. Here I was, on the precipice of adulthood, and my life was already over. I had been told that MIT was the only option for someone with my dreams, and MIT had been given to me. But as soon as I got it, it was gone. So what could I do?

I knew I could not go far. Part of the problem with MIT was the cross-country travel, which entailed more expense. So I would stay locally, in California. I could not go to Stanford; it was a private school and cost more than we could handle. But Dad always knew I would go somewhere, and he had saved what he could. He couldn't finance MIT or Stanford, but at $75 a year, the University of California, Berkeley was in reach.

At the time, UC Berkeley was not what it is now. Any student with halfway decent grades — a "B" average — would get in, and I had no problem with admission. When I enrolled, I was not happy. But I went.

During college, I lived at home. Five of us carpooled 20 minutes to campus each day; the entire cost of our commute was a quarter to get over the bridge, plus gas. I took a job to help pay the bills, and though people at Berkeley tended not to speak negatively of Japanese Americans at least when we were around, there was racial hatred around me. Japanese were no longer the most hated racial minority in California. Now, at the water cooler, people sounded off on Jews, or other groups who were becoming more visible as Japanese Americans tried to blend in. And I had to stand there, grateful it wasn't me this time.

That was true throughout my career, and my life — I always heard people spewing hate toward others whom they considered a threat. It irked me, because I had been the other as a child, when I couldn't even defend myself. I knew how it felt to be hated by everyone just for existing. I knew how it scarred you.

But back to school. I sat in lectures with 300 or 400 other students, and I did not like any of it. I was accustomed to my high school, where 20 students at a time filtered in and out of classrooms to learn. Now, we sat silently as a mass, taking notes and tests but never engaging with the material in a real way.

It wasn't until upper division courses that I got more personalized attention, and so school got better. But I will never know how it would have been at MIT, and how my life would have been shaped differently if I had been able to attend. It's true that Berkeley prides itself on building leaders, and I became one. The school gave me a good education, and of course I'm grateful. But not having the choice to create my own destiny hurt — once again, I was denied the freedom to be who I was where I wanted to be, a trend that still traced back to when I was 9 years old and loaded onto a bus to Pomona.

Nevertheless, I did just fine. My career thrived. Fresh out of college, I had six offers from major aerospace engineering companies, all of which included massive salaries. At the recommendation of a Berkeley professor, I landed at Douglas Aircraft Company, which after a series of mergers has now become Boeing. All of this opportunity was thanks to others who came before me — two black men who demanded FDR sign an executive order against discrimination in defense industries during the first years of the Second World War. While I was in captivity, aerospace engineering was in the process of diversifying. And by the time I got out and was ready to be recruited, these industries were in turn ready for me.

That doesn't mean that everyone was as accepting. As I searched for my first home, I visited neighborhoods where I would want to live in houses I knew I could afford. When landlords saw me in-person, they would tell me the property I was interested in was no longer available. Or, they would be blunter: "There's only one other family like yours in this neighborhood," they said. They did not mean engineers, or Berkeley graduates, or California natives. They meant Japanese people.

So I kept my head low, focused on work, and became successful. I got a master's at UCLA. I became one of the few executives at Boeing who were Japanese. And I learned to be happy, after so many years.

From the ashes of imprisonment, I emerged a rocket scientist. I survived one of America's worst blights on its human rights record, and I came out stronger.

But that wasn't true for everyone. I know a friend whose father killed himself for insurance money when he couldn't find a job. I've met others who lost their loved ones to suicide, who still don't want to share their stories because of how much they hurt. I know lives that were never able to restack the blocks in their favor. And that was the government's fault, but it was also ours. As American citizens, no matter color or creed, we all should have known better. We should have done something.

Please — I beg you — do something now.

Part 4: Getting Up

Eureka (I Found It)

Vague memories of a young Helene Hideno Nakamoto float around the corners of my mind. She was roughly two years younger than I was. We attended the same grammar school, but to me, she was so childish, so small. We were not on the same plane, she and I. I was one of the big kids, and she was just a 7-year-old girl with so much to learn about the world.

She no doubt learned it quickly when she and her family were shipped off to Utah, where they spent years in another internment camp hours away from Heart Mountain. And when she and I came back to San Francisco, we had both aged and changed. That was when I noticed her.

Wednesday nights were the happening time in San Francisco's Japantown. All of the teenagers assembled for choir practice, and while our parents assumed we were singing hymns and other songs of worship, we stole the moments we could to flirt with the girls and boys around us. Helene was there. I don't remember her voice, nor mine, but we sang well enough to survive the choir.

What I do remember is the nights out for sodas. Sometimes, she and I would go alone. Other times, we'd have friends join us. Everything back then had to be proper, supervised. It was the era of "I Love Lucy" and "The Ed Sullivan Show," and as Americans, we fit into that tableau of good boys and girls.

Once we got to high school, Helene and I saw each other less. She went to public school while I was at Lick-Wilmerding, and our social circles were scrambled. But I still saw her when I could. Once, I borrowed her father's car so we could visit relatives elsewhere in California. Another vehicle rammed into us from the back, and I had to explain to her dad why his car ended up totaled under my supervision.

I would not say we ever dated. We went out, but there was no going steady, no commitment or promises. I went out with other girls, too, especially when I was at Berkeley and she stayed in San Francisco for college. But when it came time to carve my own path, I knew who I wanted beside me. As my time at Berkeley drew to a close, so did my time alone.

I graduated on June 6. On June 10, Helene and I got married. And four days later, on June 14, I started at Douglas Aircraft Company. Our honeymoon was so short because we were young and broke, and there was no time to celebrate. I needed to make money so my new family could survive.

Things were very different a decade later. A successful engineer, I could provide for us just fine; there was even money left over after all the bills were paid. It was then, in the 1960s, that we got a call. One of our relatives had been to an exhibition at the Smithsonian, and she had recognized a face. Not of a staffer, or another visitor strolling the hallways, looking at art. She saw a photograph of a little girl in 1940s San Francisco, and she swore she knew her. She swore it was Helene.

Back then, you couldn't just Google an artist or send each other pictures in real time. But this relative was so sure of that face, so sure it was my wife looking back at her. And we had to see for ourselves.

Helene and I hopped on a plane to Washington, D.C., where the Smithsonian waited for us. The exhibit, we were told, was on the third floor. As we climbed the steps to the National Museum of American History, we were shocked. Helene's face was plastered on the stairwell walls — just hers. Again and again. Every few feet, she stared back at us, showing us where to go. Her big, solemn eyes were much too serious for a girl of 7, but they had to be. They were at work. She was trying to tell us something.

When we arrived at the exhibit, there she was again — this time blown up large. Little Helene stood surrounded by classmates and friends reciting the Pledge of Allegiance at our grammar school. With one hand over her heart and another clutching a brown paper lunch bag, she looked fixedly upward, like she was praying. But if she was praying, it was to our Constitution, and our Bill of Rights, and our Union. It was a devoted prayer to the sanctity of the United States of America, and this little girl was a high priestess for democracy.

The portrait was titled "Salute of Innocence." Whoever curated the collection had decided to overlay photo with the preamble to the U.S. Constitution, and the message was clear. What had happened to us had been unconstitutional.

Before I stepped into the Smithsonian, I suppose I knew that something bad had happened to me, something wrong. But it took seeing my wife reciting the Pledge of Allegiance just before she was interned to shake me enough so that I knew my civil rights had been violated. Hers, too. In fact, the civil rights of 120,000 people had been run over like they were nothing, like basic human decency did not matter as long as there was fear to trample it.

Courtesy of the National Archives/ Dorothea Lange

That photo, "Salute of Innocence," was our family's first introduction to Dorothea Lange. She was so good at her craft that we had not noticed her lingering around our school as children. My wife — her poster child — did not even remember having her photo taken. But thank goodness Dorothea was there. She created a record for those of us who were too young to know what happened. She documented who we were and what happened to us not only so the rest of America could look back and see what they did, but so that one day I could stand in the Smithsonian with my wife and understand. Without Ms. Lange, I may have never known why I was so mad, why I felt so much resentment. But with her photo, all the warped anger came into focus. Every single little girl in that photo said the Pledge of Allegiance as a way to show they loved their country. And weeks later, they were on a bus to a place where they would be treated like livestock.

In shock, Helene and I left the exhibit to explore the gift shop. And there she was again, on a collectable poster — the kind college students put on their walls. She wanted to keep it. It would represent a memento of something unexpected. It would represent revelation, epiphany. And it would represent her, before everything. Before she learned the pledge had lied to us.

Helene took the poster to the store clerk. "This is me," she said, pointing at her 7-year-old self. "May I please have it?"

"Sure," the clerk said. "For $10.50."

Return to Heart Mountain

I swore I would never go back to Wyoming. When we left Heart Mountain, I knew I would hate that land forever, as it had hated me. I remembered the people in Cody — the look of loathing in their eyes, and those signs that singled me out as unwanted. And I promised myself to detest them just as they had me, because who wants to be somewhere they're not welcome?

As I grew older, my resentment toward the American people and this government dissipated. I was a man now, and true men shouldn't isolate any section of their heart for hate. It's not worth the space. But even as I learned to forgive most of the people who had unwittingly caused me so much pain, I could not do the same for the people of Wyoming. To me, they were racists. They deserved to feel despised, like they had made me feel as a boy.

And so I went on, resenting them for how their parents had seen me decades before. Feeling they deserved punishment like the kind inflicted upon me. I thought of them as the manifestation of this country's worst flaws, and I avoided that part of the country whenever I could.

But sometime in the 1970s, I think, my friends and I decided to take a bus tour. The aim was to end up in Yellowstone, but to do that we would have to go from North Dakota through to Wyoming. I didn't think much of it, until one of our stops was in Cody. From town, I could see Heart Mountain looming above, and something came over me. I had to bear witness to what was left.

"Would it be okay to get off here?" I asked our tour guide. He said it was fine. A few of us rented a car and drove to that place I had sworn off long ago, that had haunted every step of my life since I was a child.

When we got there, we tracked down a woman who was able to take us on a tour of the grounds. But to be honest, there wasn't all that much to see. After we had left in 1945, the government had sold off the barracks to farmers for $1 a piece. Part of the hospital was there, and a sliver of the high school. The place where we once stored our freshly grown vegetables was still intact. But otherwise, Heart Mountain was gone. The American people had been confronted by our demons, and as a society, we opted for erasure over recognition. We decided that if oppression was no longer visible, we could pretend it didn't happen.

Except it was still visible, at least to me. I asked our tour guide if she knew where Block 14 had been — my block — and she took me there. Then, I asked for Barrack 22, my barrack. She knew exactly where it had stood. The place where I had suffered for three years was now painted anew with a thriving cornfield, and yet, as I stood in its midst, I could see Heart Mountain, as I remembered it. All of its horrors. All of its fears. All of its boredom, and loss, and anger, and hope. And finally, I could let go.

Listen

I was enjoying retirement — traveling, seeing the world, fly fishing — when the phone rang. It felt almost like an accident. Christy Fleming was on the line. In 2011, Heart Mountain had reopened its doors as a museum and learning center, and I knew Christy as the project's manager. We met when I visited the campgrounds to watch reconstruction. She must have dug deep into her address book to come up with my name.

I will never know why she chose me. What matters is she did.

"We've had a request for a speaker," Christy said. "Can you speak?"

Well, could I? I had spoken throughout my career at Boeing, so I supposed I could. But I had never shared my story of imprisonment publicly — I had never allowed the world to get that close.

"Sure," I said, "I can speak."

I would be presenting to a group of attorneys from the Department of Justice, she said, and I knew I needed to bone up on my knowledge before I did. Personal anecdote is not enough; it's the power of history that sways us. And so I learned about Executive Order 9066, which made it possible for Lieutenant General DeWitt to round us up and send us to prison. And I dove deep into the stories of Fred Korematsu, and Mitsuye Endo after that. I had lived every moment at Heart Mountain and suffered for the sins of my ancestry, but I had never thought to look into why.

As I studied the background — my background — what had happened became very clear: It was all about racial hatred.

The Supreme Court cases struck me especially. I spoke to the attorney who had worked on the Korematsu case, and as details began to pile up, I was struck by the lie the government constructed. When the court ruled that Japanese Americans could be interned, they essentially said that protection against espionage was more important than civil rights. I balked at that. Point me to the spy! Point me to the Japanese American who was committing espionage. Then I might understand. But to this day, I have yet to hear of a single Japanese American who was convicted of spying. We were interned because the color of our skin meant we "might" try something, and in the throes of war, fear trumped reason to make that "might" a crime.

And so I learned. And then I shared. The time finally came when I was supposed to speak to government attorneys and their staff. I decided to start my lecture with a question.

"Who here has heard of the Fred Korematsu case?" I asked.

Blank stares looked back at me. At the very rear of the room, a few hands shot up. They belonged to the youngest people there, it seemed. Everyone else was suddenly frozen.

So these were the government's lawyers, and they did not even know about Fred Korematsu, I thought. This will be easy, this'll be duck soup. Because I knew a little, and a little was a lot more than the knowledge of those around me.

After about an hour, my lecture was over. I had given the overview of what happened — a Sparknotes version — and everyone was transfixed. They had not known. The group's head immediately got out his laptop and emailed the rest of the DOJ staff that they must hear Mr. Mihara's story. My story.

That's how I became a national lecturer. It all began with a chance phone call and a meeting with 100 people from the government. And now, I believe I'm the only survivor of the camps touring the United States to talk about what we lived and witnessed.

When I started giving talks, I fielded questions about our government today. It was when I learned that we still hold children in detention that I became truly interested. I was swept back to 1942, when I was rounded up and jailed, and I thought, here we go again. People are struggling in our country, and other people don't know. I certainly hadn't known, before it was brought to my attention.

The people being detained today aren't Japanese, nor are they U.S. citizens. They're often times Central Americans seeking asylum from gang violence, state persecution and domestic abuse in their home countries. They entered our southern border and were taken into custody. And then they were put into detention centers while they awaited their hearings.

In 2014, we had what has been labeled an "immigration crisis," when women and children poured into our country. We needed places to hold them, and one of those places was built in Dilley, Texas. It was massive — able to hold thousands of family members — and to me, it sounded just like Heart Mountain. And so I decided to go and see.

I called the public affairs officer for the South Texas Family Residential Center and told her I would like to go inside. "Well, what do you do?" she asked. I told her I was a lecturer. That was not enough for her. She asked what I lectured on. And so I told her.

"Mass imprisonment," I said.

Her tone immediately changed. "We are not a prison," she said.

I was not allowed inside the detention center, but I still had to bear witness. And so I flew down to Texas and walked around the building's facade, and the parallels struck hard.

Most people would be focused on how someone might get out. But I knew how unlikely that was. And so I looked at what kept someone in. A barrier that must have been 15 feet tall stood between toddlers and their freedom. And to me, it looked an awful lot like a prison, no matter what the public affairs officer said.

Later on, I met with attorneys who represented the families detained at the South Texas Family Residential Center. They described the high security protocols at the center, and to me they sounded familiar — like a federal prison I had visited in California. I saw photos of children marching to class or the mess hall escorted by guards, and in them I saw myself. It was me, again, except this time it was another child. We were all interchangeable, because we were all the same in the eyes of the people who held us.

After my trip to Texas, I became even more interested in our immigration system. And so I visited an adult-only detention center in Eloy, Arizona. This time, I got to go inside. I spoke to some of the people who had been detained there; one of them told me he had a severe infection but the nurse practitioner would only give him painkillers. No antibiotics. No real treatment. That was like Heart Mountain, too, I thought. That had been my life.

I wish I could say these people's suffering is worth it — that they suffer for a reason. But the truth is, most of the immigrants I met at Eloy were not granted asylum. They were deported back to the countries they had fled. I feel certain that at least one of them is dead already — he had fled his country after his brother was murdered by gang members, and as soon as he returned home, I know in my heart that he met the same fate.

As I heard more, I started telling more than just my own story. Now, I try to tell the story of anybody who has ever been put away, hidden from the world so they won't cause trouble. I have spoken to elementary school children, college students, and attorneys at major law firms. Almost always, the reaction is one of shock. People do not know we were interned during World War II. Most schools have skipped over this part of American history, and most people just want to know how it felt. How did it feel to be imprisoned because of my ethnicity? How did I feel? The question is familiar, but this time, people actually want to know the answer.

Of course, I have sometimes stumbled upon individuals who think what happened to me was justified. Senior lawyers who say, "You have to understand the circumstances in 1942." I hate that expression —"you have to understand." It makes it seem as though I'm too dense to grasp the bigger picture, to take into account the major decisions Franklin D. Roosevelt and his colleagues made during a transformative time in American history. But I'm not. I do understand. More than that, I lived it. I was there. And in my understanding, what happened was not only perverse and unethical, but also unconstitutional. As protectors of the law, every attorney should care about that.

Most people are far more sympathetic. The young children in elementary school want to know details — was I ever shot at? Did I ever escape? Their questions make imprisonment seem like a movie, sexy with twists and turns, but I don't mind.

Then, as my audiences get older, their questions suddenly become more serious. This is one I get a lot:

"How do we make sure this doesn't happen again?" people ask, over and over.

And the answer is simple: We don't let it. We vote. We run for office. We care.

We listen.

Afterword

I was at Boeing during the Cold War. Some of what I made was for civilians — satellites in space for mass communication and prototypes for the first cell phones. But other Boeing projects were aimed at strengthening our military defense, and I worked on those, too. As I bolstered the U.S. arsenal, I never thought twice.

By the time I was a professional engineer, the men who had sent me to Heart Mountain were in graves. I did feel resentment toward them, but to me, they didn't represent America. There was a new wave of politicians who had replaced the old guard: John F. Kennedy and Camelot took over the Oval Office, and with them came the promise of a more tolerant, open-minded American people. We were young again, and we would not let fear control us.

With new leaders and vision, the United States once again shone as a beacon of freedom, and I never felt torn about helping our government. I wanted my skills to help promote peace, and I wanted to personally contribute to our national security. My bitterness toward the United States had mostly vanished as the '50s became the '60s, which in turn became the '70s. I refused to judge all of America as a generalized swathe, like some officials had judged the Japanese years before.

Times were changing, and I let them. That's not to say that rancor never itched at the corners of my mind. I felt wronged for decades, both by the men who had condemned me, and by some of the people of Wyoming who had looked at me like I was a criminal.

But that anger subsided, too. I learned I was wrong. Even the people of Wyoming could change after World War II hysteria lost its power, and my hatred for them was no more righteous than the hatred previous generations had felt for me. And so I let that go, too.

As the new millennium approached, wounds began to heal. The Cold War ended, and perestroika meant that tolerance spread to even the most intolerant parts of the world. Two presidents, Ronald Reagan and George H.W. Bush, apologized in writing to us for the horrors we faced during World War II, finally admitting the U.S. government's misstep, and we were paid modest reparations for the years we lost. Meanwhile, I grew older and wiser as I learned not to let my past dictate my present.

A few years ago, when we opened a learning center where Heart Mountain used to be, every store in Cody put up a sign, "Welcome Japanese Americans." And so the wrongest of the wrongs had been righted, in its own way.

Still, Heart Mountain has a legacy — one that Americans too easily forget. 120,000 Japanese living in the United States were forced to leave their homes for prisons they never deserved, but today, only a few of us are still here to remember. Our stories have not been told as often as others. And "Japanese internment" does not harbor the same psychological potency as other man-made tragedies like the Holocaust, partly because its history has faced an erasure.

I have forgiven America for what it did to my family, but I refuse to let it forget. Because once we decide to distance ourselves from a part of our past, it is too easy to repeat the mistakes that took us down a dangerous path before. Registries. Detention centers. Racism. Religious segregation. They still exist here in the United States, and their victims still suffer. Our brands of prejudice today may feel normal to us, just as Japanese internment felt normal to Americans in 1942. But they aren't, and if we don't recognize that now, future generations will judge us harshly.

There is another nine-year-old boy somewhere in America right now. He has been thrust into detention because he and his immigrant family are unwanted by our government — by our country. As he stares at stark white walls, he has learned to adapt to a new normal, though every day he longs to leave what lies behind his fence.

He is me. And you can still save us.

Appendix

Important events for Japanese Imprisonment in the United States of America

Compiled by Sam Mihara

Gentlemen's Agreement, 1907 – 1908: In San Francisco at the turn of the century, there were segregated public schools, and there was strong anti-Japanese sentiment throughout California, especially with the rising numbers of Japanese immigrant workers. Meanwhile, the Japanese government wanted Japanese Americans to attend desegregated schools. So there was an agreement between Japan and the United States to restrict the number of Japanese labor immigrants moving stateside. And in turn, schools were desegregated.

Source: Daniels, Roger. Asian America: Chinese and Japanese in the United States since 1850. Seattle: University of Washington Press, 1988.

Alien Land Laws, circa 1913: American hatred against the Japanese in the early-1900s was strong, and there were government efforts to limit the number of immigrants from Japan. Some of the regulations, the alien land laws, prohibited Japanese immigrants from purchasing or leasing property. First enacted in California in 1913, they had a huge impact on the first generation Japanese immigrants (Issei). Alien land laws were ruled unconstitutional by the U.S. Supreme Court in 1952.

Source: Lazarus, Mark. "An Historical Analysis of Alien Land Law: Washington Territory and State:

1853-1889," University of Puget Sound Law Review, 12 (1989): 198-246.

Immigration Act of 1917: A literacy test was added to the immigration process. Wives, fathers or grandfathers over the age of 55, mothers and grandmothers regardless of age, and unmarried or widowed daughters of the presumptively male immigrant or citizen were exempt from the literacy test. The Immigration Restriction League, founded in 1894, was one of the most outspoken advocates for the creation of a literacy test for immigration.

Immigration Act of 1924: This act barred immigrants from Japan and restricted the number of immigrants from Europe who could come to the United States. Supporters of the bill focused on foreigners as threats to jobs and wages. One of the act's supporters was James D. Phelan, former mayor of San Francisco, who promoted the slogan, "Keep California White," in his re- election campaign for the Senate – a campaign which he lost.

Immigration Act of 1952: A Cold War measure, the 1952 Immigration Act formally ended Asian exclusion. The act allotted nominal immigration quotas to Japan and the rest of Asia, but the racial basis of these quotas limited their actual impact. It also eliminated race as a basis for naturalization, making Japanese and other foreign-born Asians eligible to become American citizens for the first time. Highly controversial in nature, the McCarran- Walter Act had to overcome widespread opposition and a presidential veto before taking effect in June 1952.

Executive Order 9066: The advisors to the president, including Secretary of War Henry Stimson, Lieutenant General John DeWitt, and Major Karl Bendetsen, recommended President Franklin D. Roosevelt sign an executive order that gave authority to the local military commanders to remove anyone based on military need. On February 19, 1942, President Roosevelt signed Executive Order 9066 to prescribe military areas from which any or all persons may be excluded. It does not name the Japanese, Germans, or Italians by race to be excluded. As a result, some 120,000 people of Japanese ancestry were removed from the western states of California, Oregon, Washington, and parts of Southern Arizona. Similar removals of Germans and Italians did not take place in the Eastern Military District, where the German submarine threat was far more severe than maritime threats from Japan on the west coast.

Sources: Commission on Wartime Relocation and Internment of Civilians. Personal Justice Denied: Report of the Commission on Wartime Relocation and Internment of Civilians. Washington, DC: U.S. Government Printing Office, 1982. Foreword by Tetsuden Kashima. Seattle: University of Washington Press, 1997. Daniels, Roger. Prisoners without Trial: Japanese Americans in World War II. New York: Hill and Wang, 1993. Irons, Peter. Justice at War: The Story of the Japanese American Internment Cases. New York: Oxford University Press, 1983.

Exclusion Orders: The head of the Western Defense Command, Lieutenant General John L. DeWitt, issued a series of orders directing the exclusion of "all persons of Japanese ancestry," including aliens and non-aliens (U.S. citizens) from specified areas of the West Coast. Initially he requested that people voluntarily move out of the designated areas. But only a few people moved voluntarily. And so Karl Bendetsen became the architect of the 99 exclusion orders, starting with the most sensitive of area, Bainbridge Island in Washington. The orders specified how and when the move would take place. Orders were posted on walls, lampposts, and other conspicuous locations where Japanese people lived. For the day of removal, the residents were instructed to "bring only what you can carry" and store the remaining goods.

Source: Robinson, Greg. A Tragedy of Democracy: Japanese Confinement in North America. New York: Columbia University Press, 2009.

Governors' Conference at Salt Lake City: The hostility in the states where the camps were to be located became intense. The federal government, on hearing of rising concerns by local residents and state governors, called a meeting in Salt Lake City. The meeting was attended by the governors and representatives of affected states. The states of Arizona, Colorado, Utah, Washington, Oregon, Wyoming, Montana, Idaho, New Mexico, and Nevada were all represented. The federal government was represented by Milton Eisenhower, the younger brother of Dwight D. Eisenhower. He started the meeting by explaining the purpose of the camps and the fact that the Japanese were not prisoners and would be encouraged to move out and resettle in other parts of the country. The plan was not to create a prison condition. On hearing of the government's plan, the governors verbally objected. Idaho attorney general Bert Miller advocated that "all Japanese be put in concentration camps, for the remainder of the war." Arizona governor Sidney Osborn said, "We do not propose to be made a dumping ground for enemy aliens from any other state... I cannot too strongly urge that such aliens be placed in concentration camps east of the Rocky Mountains." Wyoming governor Nels Smith said that his state would not "stand for being California's dumping ground." If Japanese Americans bought land in his state, he added, "There would be Japs hanging from every pine tree." The only partial exception to this perspective came from Colorado's governor Ralph Carr, who said, "If Colorado's part in the war is to take 100,000 of them, then Colorado will take care of them," a position that would contribute to his not being reelected. As Eisenhower summarized, "The consensus of the meeting (was) that the plan for reception centers was acceptable to the states so long as the evacuees remained within the reception centers under guard. Concentration camps, it would have to be."

Sources: Roger Daniels, "Report on the Salt Lake City meeting from the Records of the Secretary of Agriculture." In American Concentration Camps: Volume 4, April, 1942. New York: Garland Publishing, 1989. Irons, Peter. Justice at War: The Story of the Japanese American Internment Cases. New York: Oxford University Press, 1983. de Nevers, Klancy Clark. The Colonel and the Pacifist: Karl Bendetsen, Perry Saito and the Incarceration of Japanese

Americans during World War II. Forward by Roger Daniels. Salt Lake City: University of Utah Press, 2004.

Loyalty Questionnaire: In 1943, the government decided to implement an examination of all adult residents of the Japanese internment camps to determine their loyalty to the United States. This "Loyalty Questionnaire" included 28 questions which required a simple "yes" or "no" response. The primary purpose was to help the government identify those who were eligible for recruiting into an all Japanese-American military combat unit. Question number 27 asked if Nisei men were willing to serve on combat duty wherever ordered and asked everyone else if they would be willing to serve in other ways, such as joining the Women's Army Auxiliary Corps. Question number 28 asked if individuals would swear unqualified allegiance to the United States and forswear any form of allegiance to the Emperor of Japan. Citizens resented being asked to renounce loyalty to the Emperor of Japan when they had never held a loyalty to the Emperor. Also, Japanese immigrants were barred from becoming U.S. citizens on the basis of race, so renouncing their only citizenship was problematic, leaving them stateless. Inmates who refused to give unqualified "yes" responses were segregated to Tule Lake, California, and unjustly labeled as "disloyal."

Sources: Hayashi, Brian Masaru. Democratizing the Enemy: The Japanese American Internment. Princeton, N.J.: Princeton University Press, 2004. Lyon, Cherstin. Prisons and Patriots: Japanese American Wartime Citizenship, Civil Disobedience, and Historical

Memory. Philadelphia: Temple University Press, 2011. Muller, Eric. *American Inquisition: The Hunt for Japanese American Disloyalty in World War II.* Chapel Hill: University of North Carolina Press, 2007. Omori, Emiko. *Rabbit in the Moon.* Hohokus, N.J.: New Day Films, 1999. Weglyn, Michi. *Years of Infamy: The Untold Story of America's Concentration Camps.* Seattle: University of Washington Press, 1996.

Tule Lake: Tule Lake became the largest War Relocation Authority (WRA) concentration camp, with a peak population of 18,789 inmates. Security at the Tule Lake site was increased when it became a segregation center. More barbed wire was added and an eight-foot high double "man-proof" fence was constructed to secure the maximum-security segregation center. The six guard towers surrounding the site were increased to 28, and a battalion of 1,000 military police with armored cars and tanks was brought in to maintain security. A handful of inmates were picked up by WRA internal security and savagely beaten before being turned over to the military police and imprisoned in the "bullpen" area of the hastily assembled stockade. Tule Lake became an armed camp with a prisoner curfew, barrack-to-barrack searches, and a near complete cessation of normal activities. Martial law was declared on November 14, leading to months of repression and hardship. In February 1946, a contingent of 4,406 Tule Lake inmates voluntarily left for Japan, including 1,116 renunciants, 1,523 aliens and 1,767 U.S. citizens, the latter consisting mostly of children and adolescents.

Sources: Collins, Donald E. *Native American Aliens: Disloyalty and the Renunciation of Citizenship by Japanese Americans during World War II.* Westport, CN: Greenwood Press, 1985. Drinnon, Richard. *Keeper of Concentration Camps: Dillon S. Myer and American Racism.* Berkeley: University of California Press, 1987. *From a Silk Cocoon.* Video. Produced by Satsuki Ina. 90 min. 2005. Kashima, Tetsuden. *Judgment without Trial: Japanese American Imprisonment during World War II.* Seattle: University of Washington Press, 2003. Kashiwagi, Hiroshi. *Shoe Box Plays.* San Mateo, CA: Asian American Curriculum Project, 2008. Kumei, Teruko. "Skeleton in the Closet: The Japanese American Hokoku Seinen-dan and Their 'Disloyal' Activities at the Tule Lake Segregation Center during World War II." *Japanese Journal of American Studies* 7 (1996): 67–102. Nakagawa, Martha. "Renunciants: Bill Nishimura and Tad Yamakido." *Journal of the Shaw Historical Library* 19 (2005): 137–59. National Park Service, Tule Lake Unit. http://www.nps.gov/tule. Ross, John, and Reiko Ross. *Second Kinenhi: Reflections on Tule Lake.* San Francisco: Tule Lake Committee, 2000. Takei, Barbara. "Legalizing Detention: Segregated Japanese Americans and the Justice Department's Renunciation Program." *Journal of the Shaw Historical Library* 19 (2005): 75–105. Takei, Barbara, and Judy Tachibana. *Tule Lake Revisited, Second Edition.* San Francisco: Tule Lake Committee, 2012. Tule Lake Committee. http://www.tulelake.org. Weglyn, Michi. *Years of Infamy: The Untold Story of America's Concentration Camps.* New York: William Morrow and Co., 1976.

Military Service: Japanese Americans served in the military during WWII. They mostly served in the segregated 442nd Regimental Combat Team and its predecessor, the 100th Infantry Battalion in Europe. Others served as translators and interpreters in the Military Intelligence Service. To build up forces for the war, the initial call for volunteers went out to both Hawaii and the camps. The Hawaiian volunteers totaled more than 10,000, out of which 2,686 were accepted. But in the mainland camps there were barely 1,000 volunteers. In all, the 100th and 442nd received 9,486 Purple Hearts, eight Presidential Unit Citations, 559 Silver Stars, and 52 Distinguished Service Crosses, among many other decorations. In the immediate aftermath of the war, only one member of the 442nd regiment received the Medal of Honor, America's highest military honor. However, a review in the 1990s resulted in 20 additional Medals of Honors being awarded in 2000. Among the decorations received by the MIS are a Presidential Unit Citation, five Silver Stars, and three Distinguished Service Crosses. An estimated 33,000 Japanese Americans served in the military during and immediately after World War II, about 18,000 in the 442nd and 6,000 as part of the MIS. Approximately 800 Japanese Americans were killed-in-action during World War II.

Sources: 100th Infantry Battalion Veterans Education Center.www.100thbattalion.org/. Americans of Japanese Ancestry World War II Memorial Alliance. http://www.ajawarvets.org/mainmenu.cfm?stg=home. Duus, Masayo. Unlikely Liberators: The Men of the 100th and the 442nd. Honolulu: University of Hawaii

Press, 1987. Go For Broke National Education Center. http://www.goforbroke.org/. Hawaii Nikkei History Editorial Board. Japanese Eyes...American Heart: Personal Reflections of Hawaii's World War II Nisei Soldiers. Honolulu: Tendai Educational Foundation, 1998. The Hawaii Nisei Story: Americans of Japanese Ancestry during World War II. http://nisei.hawaii.edu/page/home. Japanese American Veterans Association. http://www.javadc.org/main.htm. Odo, Franklin S. No Sword to Bury: Japanese Americans in Hawaii during World War II. Philadelphia: Temple University Press, 2003. Shirey, Orville C. Americans: The Story of the 442nd Combat Team. Washington, D.C.: Infantry Journal Press, 1946. Tanaka, Chester. Go for Broke: A Pictorial History of the Japanese American 100th Infantry Battalion and the 442nd Regimental Combat Team. Richmond, CA: Go for Broke, Inc., 1981. Novato, CA: Presidio Press, 1997.

Draft Resistance: Not all military draft subjects willingly joined the military. There was resistance to conscription into the United States Army under the Selective Service and Training Act of 1940 by nearly 300 incarcerated Japanese Americans. Draft resisters came from eight of the 10 War Relocation Authority Camps, with the largest numbers coming from Poston and Heart Mountain. In both camps, the issue of draft resistance surged to the forefront of public discussion. With 106 resisters, Poston had the largest overall number at any of the camps, but it was also by far the most populous camp. Heart Mountain's 85 resisters gave it the distinction of the highest rate of resistance.

Following federal trials for resisting the draft, most resisters served time in federal prison for their resistance. Later, after their release from prison, President Harry S. Truman signed a pardon for all resisters who were sent to prison. To show that the issue was not a question of loyalty, many went on to serve in the military during the Korean War.

Sources: Cherstin Lyon. Prisons and Patriots: Japanese American Wartime Citizenship, Civil Disobedience, and Historical Memory. Philadelphia: Temple University Press, 2011. Eric L. Muller. Free to Die for their Country: The Story of the Japanese American Draft Resisters in World War II. Chicago: University of Chicago Press, 2001.

Fred Korematsu Case: There were three landmark Supreme Court cases concerning wartime civil liberties. Three Nisei elected to not follow the orders to be removed from homes in the west coast – Fred Korematsu, Gordon Hirabayashi and Minoru Yasui. Fred Korematsu was a welder in the Oakland Naval Shipyards, where he was terminated shortly after December 7, 1941. Fred had an Italian-American girlfriend, and they decided to evade the forced removal and stay on the west coast. Fred had plastic surgery and changed his name to appear non-Japanese. He was caught, went to trial and found guilty of violating the removal orders. After the federal district court in San Francisco found him guilty of violating military orders, his case went to the U.S. Supreme Court in 1944. The high court upheld the lower court's ruling in a 6-3 vote. In the 1980s, legal historian and author Peter Irons filed a petition—called the writ of coram nobis—to the 9th U.S. Circuit Court in San Francisco to have Korematsu's conviction overturned on the grounds that the Supreme Court had made its decision based on false information. In November 1983, U.S. District Judge Marilyn Hall Patel vacated Korematsu's conviction and argued that the Korematsu case serves as a "caution that in times of distress the shield of military necessity and national security must not be used to protect governmental actions from close scrutiny and accountability."

Sources: Alonso, Karen. Korematsu v. United States: Japanese American Internment Camps. Berkeley Heights, New Jersey: Enslow Publishers, 1998. Korematsu Institute for Civil Rights and Education. "Fred Korematsu Bio." http://korematsuinstitute.org/institute/aboutfred/. Yamamoto, Eric and May Lee. "Excerpts from a Brief Biography: Fred Korematsu". Asian American Bar Association of the Greater Bay Area. http://www.aaba-bay.com/aaba/showpage.asp?code=yamamotoarticle.

Gordon Hirabayashi and Minoru Yasui Cases: Gordon Hirabayashi lived in Seattle, Washington. He was raised as a religious pacifist, and he knew his rights as an American citizen. He registered with the Selective Service as a conscientious objector and joined the Religious Society of Friends, otherwise known as the Quakers. Gordon elected to not follow curfew orders and told the authorities he planned not to comply with the removal orders. Hirabayashi was indicted on May 28, 1942 for violating Public Law No. 505, which made violating Civilian Exclusion Order No. 57 and curfew a federal crime. He was found guilty and ordered to serve time in prison. The case was sent to the U.S. Supreme Court, which made a unanimous ruling in Hirabayashi v. United States (320 U.S. 81) upholding Hirabayashi's conviction on June 21, 1943. Years later, shortly after retirement as a faculty member at the University of Alberta, Hirabayashi received a call from Peter Irons inviting him to allow a team of lawyers to re-open his wartime conviction on the basis of governmental misconduct. The Ninth Circuit Court of Appeals ruled in favor of Hirabayashi's coram nobis case, vacating his personal conviction in 1987.

Sources: Hirabayashi, Gordon K., James A. Hirabayashi, and Lane Ryo Hirabayashi. A Principled Stand: Gordon Hirabayashi versus the United States. Seattle: University of Washington Press, forthcoming, 2013. Irons, Peter. Justice at War. New York: Oxford University Press, 1983. Lyon, Cherstin. Prisons and Patriots: Japanese American Wartime Citizenship, Civil Disobedience, and Historical Memory. Philadelphia: Temple University Press, 2011.

Minoru Yasui Case: Minoru Yasui was born and raised in Hood River, Oregon, to immigrant parents who were fruit farmers. Yasui attended the University of Oregon for his bachelor's degree and went on to earn his law degree there in 1939, becoming the first Japanese American to graduate from Oregon's law school. When travel restrictions and curfews were established against Japanese Americans, he decided to make himself a legal test case. On March 28, 1942,

Yasui walked through downtown Portland after 8 p.m., deliberately breaking curfew. When no one noticed, he approached a policeman and demanded to be arrested. He was only told to go home. So he marched into the police station and demanded to be arrested, where the officer on duty obliged. Yasui was ultimately convicted in his challenge of the curfew and lost his appeal in front of the Supreme Court.

Sources: Hosokawa, Bill. Colorado's Japanese Americans from 1886 to the Present. Boulder: University Press of Colorado, 2005. Irons, Peter. Justice at War: The Story of the Japanese American Internment Cases. New York: Oxford University Press, 1983. Berkeley: University of California Press, 1993.

Mitsuye Endo Case: A San Francisco attorney, James Purcell, filed a lawsuit on behalf of Mitsuye Endo, a prisoner at one of the concentration camps. Seeking a test case for whom he could file a habeas corpus petition, he settled on Endo without actually meeting her based on her profile as a Nisei who was Christian, had a brother in the U.S. Army, had never been to Japan, and could neither speak nor read Japanese. Endo agreed to serve as the test case. Purcell's main argument was that the constitution states a U.S. citizen who is loyal and has no prior record of crimes or suspected crimes cannot be held in detention. In a unanimous ruling issued on December 18, 1944, the court decided in Endo's favor. The opinion, authored by Justice William O. Douglas, began: "We are of the view that Mitsuye Endo should be given her liberty. In reaching that conclusion we do not come to the underlying constitutional issues which have been argued. For we conclude that, whatever power the War Relocation Authority may have to detail other classes of citizens, it has no authority to subject citizens who are concededly loyal to its leave procedure."

Sources: Ex Parte Mitsuye Endo, 323 U.S. 283 (1944) case transcript, http://caselaw.lp.findlaw.com/cgi-bin/getcase.pl?court=us&vol=323&invol=283.
Gudridge, Patrick O. "Remember Endo?" Harvard Law Review 116 (2003): 1933–70. Irons, Peter. Justice at War: The Story of the Japanese American Internment Cases. New York: Oxford University Press, 1983. Berkeley: University of California Press, 1993. Kang, Jerry. "Denying Prejudice: Internment, Redress, and Denial." UCLA Law Review 51.4 (2004): 933–1013. Muller, Eric. "An Online Mini-Symposium Commemorating the Life of Mitsuye Endo, a Quiet Civil Rights Hero." Is That Legal? Blog, http://www.isthatlegal.org/archives/2006/06/this_wee k_at_is.html.

Redress and Civil Liberties Act of 1988: The Redress Movement refers to efforts to obtain the restitution of civil rights, an apology, and monetary compensation from the U.S. government during the six decades that followed the World War II mass removal and confinement of Japanese Americans. Early campaigns emphasized the violation of constitutional rights, lost property, and the repeal of anti-Japanese legislation. 1960s activists linked the wartime detention camps to contemporary racist and colonial policies. In the late-1970s, three organizations pursued redress in court and in Congress, culminating in the passage of the Civil Liberties Act of 1988, providing a national apology and individual payments of $20,000 to surviving detainees.

The Commission on the Wartime Internment and Relocation of Civilians (CWRIC): Congress and President Jimmy Carter approved the creation of a Commission on Wartime Relocation and Internment of Civilians (CWRIC) in 1980. This bipartisan commission held 20 days of hearings with more than 750 witnesses and spent a year and a half researching scholarship and archival sources. More than 500 former detainees testified. Their accounts of pain and suffering galvanized redress support from Japanese Americans who attended the hearings or read excerpts of testimony in newspapers and magazines. JACL leaders and members testified at every hearing location and consistently urged the Commission to recommend that Congress provide an apology and compensation of $25,000 to each person who suffered exclusion and detention. The Commission's 1983 report acknowledged the injustice of mass exclusion, removal and detention and concluded these policies were caused not by "military necessity" but by "race prejudice, war hysteria, and a failure of political leadership."

Sources: Commission on Wartime Relocation and Internment of Civilians. Personal Justice Denied: Report of the Commission on Wartime Relocation and Internment of Civilians. Washington, DC: Government Printing Office, 1982. Commission on Wartime Relocation and Internment of Civilians. Personal Justice Denied, Part II: Recommendations. Washington,

DC: Government Printing Office, 1983. Maki, Mitchell T., Harry H. L. Kitano, and S. Megan Berthold. Achieving the Impossible Dream: How Japanese Americans Obtained Redress. Urbana and Chicago: University of Illinois Press, 1999. Yamamoto, Eric K., et al. Race, Rights and Reparation: Law and the Japanese American Internment. Gaithersburg, NY: Aspen Publishers, 2001.

Civil Liberties Act of 1988: The federal act (Public Law 100-383) that granted redress of $20,000 and a formal presidential apology to every surviving U.S. citizen or legal resident immigrant of Japanese ancestry incarcerated during World War II. First introduced in Congress as the Civil Liberties Act of 1987 (H.R. 442) and signed into law on August 10, 1988, by President Ronald Reagan, the act cited "racial prejudice, wartime hysteria and a lack of political leadership" as causes for the incarceration as a result of formal recommendations by the Commission on Wartime Relocation and Internment of Civilians (CWRIC), a body appointed by Congress in 1980 to make findings on and suggest remedies for the incarceration.

Sources: Commission on Wartime Relocation and Internment of Civilians. Personal Justice Denied: Report of the Commission on Wartime Relocation and Internment of Civilians. Seattle: University of Washington Press and Washington D.C.: Civil Liberties Public Education Fund, 1997. Daniels, Roger. "Relocation, Redress, and the Report: A Historical Appraisal." In Japanese Americans: From Relocation to Redress, edited by Roger Daniels, Sandra C. Taylor, and Harry H.L. Kitano: 3–9. Salt Lake City: University of Utah Press, 1987. Revised edition. Seattle: University of Washington Press, 1991.

Sam Mihara

Sam Mihara is a second-generation Japanese American born and raised in San Francisco. Sam attended U.C. Berkeley undergraduate and UCLA graduate schools, where he earned engineering degrees. He became a rocket engineer and joined the Boeing Company, where he became an executive on space programs. Following retirement, Sam changed careers and is now a visiting lecturer for the University of California, Harvard Law School, and other leading schools and universities. He is also a national speaker on mass imprisonment in the United States. In 2018, he was awarded the National Council for History Education's Paul A. Gagnon Prize for his work on Heart Mountain.

Alexandra Villarreal

Born in Corpus Christi, Texas, Alexandra is a professional journalist whose work has been published in *The Associated Press*, *The Guardian*, *The New York Times*, NBC Digital, *The Philadelphia Inquirer*, and Hearst newspapers, among others. Though she counts New York City as her home, she is constantly on the move.